Dreamboat
On Word

Dreamboat on Word

Copyright © 2003 by Anne Troy

All rights reserved. No part of this book may be reproduced or transmitted in any form or by any means, electronic or mechanical, including photocopying, recording, or by any information storage retrieval system without written permission from the publisher.

Written by:
Anne Troy a/k/a "Dreamboat"

Edited by:
Tracy Syrstad

Interior Design:
Linda DeLonais

Cover Design:
Irubin Consulting

Published by:
Holy Macro! Books
13386 Judy Avenue Northwest
Uniontown, Ohio, USA 44685

Distributed by:
Independent Publishers Group

Second printing:
February 2004
Printed in the Hong Kong

Library of Congress Control Number: 2003108839

ISBN: 0-9724258-4-5

Trademarks:
All brand names and product names used in this book are trade names, service marks, trademarks, or registered trademarks of their respective owners. Holy Macro! Books is not associated with any product or vendor mentioned in this book.

About the Author

Back when most of us were still in awe of self-correcting typewriters and home PCs were the exception rather than the rule, Anne Troy was creating her own databases and teaching fellow employees how to use mail merge and create templates. Leaving the office administration field for the challenges of an IT-based career was a natural progression.

These days, her resume shows extensive experience in desktop publishing, project management for Microsoft Office VBA development, Microsoft Office Helpdesk Analyst and Trainer. All of these services are offered through her website:

www.TheOfficeExperts.com

Ms. Troy is the mother of one grown daughter and lives in Quakertown, Pennsylvania with her husband and business partner, Scott Pierson.

On the rare occasions when her hands are not flying between a keyboard and a mouse, she uses them to pick up her new grandson.

Acknowledgements

I would like to personally thank the following persons for their contributions to this book, whether the contribution was literal or encouraging and supportive. They appear in alphabetical order because I cannot list everyone in the top spot, though they all belong there.

Tom Giaquinto

Kathy Jacobs of www.PowerPointAnswers.com

Bill Jelen of www.MrExcel.com

Ken Lombardi

Suat Ozgur

Scott Pierson

Eleanor Sadorf

Malcolm Smith of www.DragonDrop.com

Tracy Syrstad

SnagIt® from www.TechSmith.com

For pushing me to be the best I can be, I want to thank all of the askers and experts at all the free tech support sites listed below, all the people at PC Helps Support, Inc., and Brainbench and the people in their MVP Program.

Free tech support sites I frequent regularly:

The Office Experts at http://www.theofficeexperts.com/forum

Tech Support Guy at http://forums.techguy.org

Experts Exchange at http://www.experts-exchange.com

Tek-Tips at http://www.tek-tips.com

Utter Access at http://www.utteraccess.com/forums

Table of Contents

1. Introduction	**1-1**
2. What's New in Word 2003?	**2-1**
Multiple Versions	2-1
Permissions	2-1
Format→Background	2-2
Styles Formatting	2-2
Getting Help on the Web	2-2
Smart Tags	2-2
Extensible Markup Language (XML)	2-2
Dictionaries and Thesauruses	2-2
Reading Layout	2-2
3. Word's Application Window	**3-1**
Menus and Toolbars	3-1
Default Menu, Toolbar and Keyboard Settings	3-1
Learn Word's Menus Quickly	3-3
Learn Word's Toolbars Quickly	3-4
Customizing Menus, Toolbars and Shortcut Settings	3-7
Customize/Modify Toolbar Buttons	3-9
Resetting Menus and Toolbars	3-10
What's With The Taskbar?	3-11
Shortcut Keys	3-11
Windows Shortcut Keys	3-11
Word Shortcut Keys	3-12
Windows Dialog Boxes	3-14
Option Settings	3-16
AutoCorrect Settings	3-17
4. Features I Love	**4-1**
Document Map	4-1
Organizer	4-2
AutoText	4-3
Purpose of AutoText Entries	4-4
Naming AutoText Entries	4-5
Sharing AutoText Entries	4-5
Find and Replace	4-6
Microsoft Equation	4-9

Dreamboat On Word   v

Table of Contents

Calculations 4-10
Format Painter 4-11
Outline View 4-12

5. Features I Could Live Without 5-1
Master/Subdocuments 5-1
    Steps to Master/Subdocuments 5-2
    Troubleshooting Master/Subdocuments 5-4
    Unlocking Master Documents 5-5
AutoFormat 5-6
Indexing 5-6
The Web Toolbar 5-7
Default Document View 5-7
Cross-References 5-7
Envelopes and Labels 5-8
    Envelopes 5-8
    Labels 5-9

6. Fonts and Formatting 6-1
Considerations 6-1
Too Many Fonts 6-2
Safe Fonts 6-2
Font Dialog Box 6-3

7. Paragraph Formatting 7-1
Indents and Spacing 7-2
    Indentation 7-2
    Special Indentation 7-5
Spacing Between Paragraphs 7-6

8. Tabs 8-1
Default Tab Settings and Potential Problems 8-2
Left-Aligned Tab 8-6
Center-Aligned Tab 8-6
Right-Aligned Tab 8-7
Decimal-Aligned Tab 8-8
Bar Tab 8-9
Using the Tab Settings Dialog Box 8-10
Leaders 8-11

9. Styles 9-1

Create a Custom Style	9-5
Sample Text	9-6
Changing Style Formatting	9-7
Creating TOCs from Styles	9-8
Style Organizer	9-9
Styles FAQ	9-11

10. Bullets and Numbering 10-1

Bullets	10-2
Numbered Lists	10-2
Outline Numbering	10-4

11. Borders and Shading 11-1

Page Borders	11-2
Other Borders	11-3
Borders in Headers and Footers	11-5

12. Tables 12-1

Creating Tables in Word	12-1
Quick Facts About Tables	12-5
When to Use	12-7
Displaying Data	12-7
Headings Left/Text Right	12-7
Lists	12-8
Headers and Footers	12-8
Creative Uses for Tables	12-9
When Not to Use Tables	12-10
Tables as Document or Manual Layouts	12-10
Tables That Have Merged Cells	12-10
Converting Tables to Text or Text to Tables	12-11

13. Section Breaks 13-1

What are Breaks for?	13-1
Types of Breaks and When to Use	13-1
Page Break	13-1
Column Break	13-3
Text Wrapping Break	13-3
Next-Page Section Break	13-3
Continuous Section Break	13-3
Even-Page Section Break	13-4
Odd-Page Section Break	13-4

Table of Contents

14. Page Numbering 14-1
Inserting Page Numbers 14-1
Formatting Page Numbers 14-2

15. Templates and Desktop Publishing 15-1
Word Templates 15-1
    Workgroup Templates 15-3
Layout Forethoughts 15-3
    Booklets and Newsletter Layouts 15-4
    Two-Sided Page Setup 15-5
Stationery Template Layouts 15-7
    Letterhead 15-8
    Envelopes 15-9
    Business Cards 15-9

16. Notes, Bookmarks, Hyperlinks and Cross-References . 16-1
Footnotes and Endnotes 16-1
    Formatting Footnotes and Endnotes 16-3
Bookmarks 16-4
    Automatic Bookmarks 16-4
Cross-References 16-5
Hyperlinks 16-5

17. Mail Merge 17-1
Main Documents 17-1
Data Sources 17-2
Using Queries 17-3
    Scenario 17-3
Conditional Mail Merges 17-5
Printing Mail Merge Documents 17-8

18. Creating Forms 18-1
Macro Button Field Forms 18-1
Fill-In Forms 18-4
    Form Fields 18-4
    Creating Forms in Tables 18-8
    Protecting Fill-In Forms 18-10
User Forms 18-12

19. Drawing in Word 19-1
Office Drawing Tools 19-1

viii   *Dreamboat On Word*

Table of Contents

    WordArt 19-2
    PhotoDraw 19-3
  Graphics and Drawing Tips..19-3
  Graphics Layout Settings 19-5
    In line with text 19-6
    Square & Tight..19-7
    Behind Text 19-7
    In Front of Text...19-7
    Float Over Text...19-8

20. Printing and Printing Issues 20-1
  Printing Page Ranges...20-1
  Blank Pages...20-3
    At the Bottom/End of the Document..20-3
    Throughout the Document..20-4
  Text Prints with Extra Space Between Letters or Words............................20-5
  Page Borders Don't Print 20-5

21. Macros and VBA 21-1
  What is a Macro? 21-1
  Macro Security 21-1
    Clean Documents of Code 21-5
  How to Record a Macro 21-8
    Step 1: Prepare to Record 21-8
    Step 2: Assign the Macro to a Toolbar Button.................................21-9
    Step 3: Record the Macro 21-11
    Step 4: Test the Macro...21-11
  Sample Word Macros...21-11
    Sample Macro 1: Return Labels to Data..21-12
    Sample Macro 2: Fun Joke and an Old Macro Virus 21-15
    Sample Macro 3: Default Open View 21-16
    Sample Macro 4: Clean All VBA Code From a Document 21-17

22. Using Word with Other Applications 22-1
  Mail Merge Data Sources 22-1
  Inserting Excel Objects..22-1
    Avoiding Problems..22-2
  Converting Word Text to PowerPoint Presentations....................................22-3
  Word as Your Outlook Email Editor 22-4

23. Important Word Files.. 23-1
  Files to Back Up..23-1

Dreamboat On Word   *ix*

Table of Contents

Normal Dot Dot 23-3
Normal.Dot Settings 23-5

24. Troubleshooting 24-1
Cleaning Your Hard Drive 24-1
    Step 1: Delete trashy hard drive files. 24-3
    Step 2: Delete Windows temp files. 24-4
    Step 3: Delete temporary Internet files. 24-5
    Step 4: Cleanup by running Scandisk and Defrag. 24-6
Physical Cleanup 24-7
    Instructions 24-7
Troubleshooting Word 24-8
    Step 1. Ensure that Word, and not the document, is the problem 24-8
    Step 2. Clean up your hard drive. 24-9
    Step 3. Rename normal.dot. 24-9
    Step 4. Check the Startup folder. 24-9
    Step 5. "Dump" the registry key. 24-11
    Step 6. Uninstall, Erase and Reinstall Office. 24-12
Troubleshooting Files 24-13
    General File Troubleshooting 24-13
    Word Document Troubleshooting 24-14
Other Common Issues 24-15
    Cannot Spell Check 24-16
    Cannot Change Text 24-16

Appendix A 1
Windows Keyboard Shortcuts 1
Recommended Settings in Word 3
Glossary 7

Index 1

Table of Tips

Tip 1: Learn Word's Menus Quickly 3-4
Tip 2: Learn Word's Toolbars Quickly 3-5
Tip 3: Customize Your Toolbars 3-8
Tip 4: Work without your Mouse 3-12
Tip 5: Print a Complete List of Word's Shortcut Keys 3-13
Tip 6: Create an AutoText Entry 4-4
Tip 7: Don't Under-Use Find & Replace 4-6
Tip 8: When to Use Master/Subdocuments 5-2
Tip 9: Fastest Method to Creating an Index 5-6
Tip 10: Fast Envelopes 5-8
Tip 11: Set the Default Font for All New Documents 6-3
Tip 12: Cautions for Using Font Formatting 6-4
Tip 13: Fix Disappearing Table Text 7-4
Tip 14: Spacing between Paragraphs 7-6
Tip 15: Using List Boxes in Dialogs 7-7
Tip 16: Using Tables instead of Tabs 8-1
Tip 17: Turning Tabbed Columns into a Data File 8-4
Tip 18: Style Hints for New Templates 9-1
Tip 19: Create a Custom Style 9-7
Tip 20: Reset Bullets and Numbering 10-1
Tip 21: Easiest Way to Fix Numbered or Bulleted Lists 10-3
Tip 22: Get Rid of Unwanted Borders 11-1
Tip 23: Borders on Headers and Footers 11-6
Tip 24: Sorting Text Without a Table 12-3
Tip 25: Avoid Odd-Page Section Breaks 13-5
Tip 26: Easiest Page Numbering Method 14-1
Tip 27: How to Set Up Typical Page Numbering Sets 14-3
Tip 28: Make Desktop Shortcuts to your Templates 15-2
Tip 29: Change a Template to a Document 15-2
Tip 30: Same Section—Multiple Documents 15-7
Tip 31: Create a Letterhead Template 15-8

Table of Contents

Tip 32: Create a Business Card Template 15-10

Tip 33: Create a Footnote or Endnote 16-2

Tip 34: Change a Footnote or Endnote Format 16-3

Tip 35: Insert Hyperlinks to Other Document Types 16-7

Tip 36: Error "A security problem has occurred." 16-8

Tip 37: Viewing the Mail Merge Toolbar (Word 2002/XP) 17-2

Tip 38: Show/Hide Field Codes 17-6

Tip 39: Correct Number and Date Formatting of Merge Fields 17-7

Tip 40: Print Only One Mail Merged Letter 17-8

Tip 41: Shading Form Fields 18-1

Tip 42: Creating Click & Type Fields 18-3

Tip 43: Creating Forms in Tables 18-9

Tip 44: Cautions on Protecting Forms 18-11

Tip 45: Creating Hyperlinks in Protected Forms 18-12

Tip 46: Working With Office Drawing Objects 19-2

Tip 47: Place Graphics In Line With Text 19-6

Tip 48: Understanding Print Range Codes 20-3

Tip 49: Minimum Margins for Your Printer 20-4

Tip 50: Avoiding Viruses 21-2

Tip 51: Setting Macro Security 21-3

Tip 52: Getting Rid of a Macro Virus 21-5

Tip 53: Stop Recording Toolbar Disappeared 21-10

Tip 54: Inserting Excel Objects Properly 22-2

Tip 55: Finding Normal.dot 23-4

Tip 56: A Caution About Troubleshooting 24-1

Tip 57: Caution About File Extensions 24-4

Tip 58: Your Windows Temp Folder 24-4

Tip 59: Recovering Lost Toolbars & Menus 24-8

Tip 60: Programs That Interfere With Word 24-10

Foreword

I'm a dinosaur! I'm fifty years old and learned to type when it was still called typing, and a keyboard was a new-fangled instrument that made all kinds of strange electronic noises. Today they call it music.

I took a course called Office Practice in high school, and Typing I and II. In Typing I you learned to type without looking at the letters. In Typing II you learned to do it faster. I could type 80 words a minute at a time when that meant something.

I worked in the legal department of a large corporation in the mid-seventies. We secretaries would sit for hours hunched over IBM Selectrics, trying to produce a "clean" first page—one with no visible corrections. We all had huge dictionaries open on our desk, and hidden bottles of WhiteOut and packs of corrections strips in our top drawers. We used carbon sheets because copying was too expensive, and our department heads frowned upon over-use of the Xerox 5700. Back then, we took dictation on steno books, and sending a fax was a major production that required permission from somebody on "mahogany row". The fax was charged to your department, as were telexes, the old-fashioned version of email.

One day the supply guy rolled in a huge machine with a noise cover and installed it at the desk of one of the girls. Training sent over a teacher who spent almost a week teaching the girl how to save her work and make corrections. It was a miracle! You could actually correct something and have it come hot off the roller as an original document!

Foreword

The world was changing, but I left to have my first child. We did that back then...actually stayed home for a few months before the big day, nesting, and then—gasp—remained home for weeks, months, even years, raising the children.

I went back to work with my little sister (you may know her as "Dreamboat") who taught me how to use a Wang word processor. I eventually got over the habit of giggling immaturely at the name, but I never really did understand what I was doing.

I've joined the techno world, but feel like I'm constantly catching up. There was a time when proficiency with a ten-key adding machine was a good thing to have on your resume. Today they're called calculators. Tell them you can take shorthand, and they think you have a physical disability. Don't stare blankly when they ask if you can mail merge or use PowerPoint, whatever the hell that is...

Every time I learn something, they teach computers how to do it for me.

Today, my little sister is self-employed in the IT business, and I'm still an administrator, though I've moved up the ladder to management. I can still type really fast without looking, but nobody cares. I can still spell, but who needs it? I can still take shorthand; but I only use it to write notes to myself.

The other day, I decided to run some errands. I started out with a stop at the MAC machine. I couldn't get any money because I couldn't remember my pin number. I went to the grocery store. The cashier asked if I would be using my super duper savings card. Sure, I said, and fished it out of my purse. Okay, she said sweetly, swipe it and enter your pin number. Never mind, I said, I don't need the groceries anyway.

If anybody wants me, I'll be in the living room, alone, staring at the weather channel. I like the weather channel. At least that's what I tell myself. Truth is, I don't know how to use the remote, and the set has been tuned to that station since 1999.

I'm sure you're wondering by now just what my point is. Well, it's this:

My little sister wrote this book. She asked me to read it just before sending it to the editor. I thought she was crazy. She's been trying to shove Word down my throat for years, but I agreed anyway. I was shocked. I actually understand this book.

Now that you know me—trust me, if I can understand this book, anyone can.

~Eleanor Sadorf
Marlborough Township, Pennsylvania
June 2003

This page left intentionally blank.

1. Introduction

Microsoft Word has the market on Word Processing software. I have heard that its share is ninety percent. The rest is made up of WordPerfect and several free or very inexpensive alternatives.

This book is for the ninety percent who use Microsoft Word, whether by choice or at gunpoint.

This entire book, except its cover, was written and designed using all of the proper layout procedures in Microsoft Word. I'd like to think that, with the help of this book, you could just as easily create a document like it.

Though Word 97 is great if you still have it, our primary focus is on versions Word 2000 and 2002/XP. For your information, the versions are referred to as described in the following table. I've included older versions for reference only.

Name	Office Version	Number
Word 6	Office 4.3*	Unknown to me
Word 7	Office 95	7.0
Word 97	Office 97	8.0
Word 2000	Office 2000	9.0
Word 2002/XP	Office 2002/XP	10.0
Word 2003	Office 11	11.0

Office 4.3 came with Access 2.0, Excel 5.0, PowerPoint 4.0, and Word 6.0. With the release of Office 95, the version numbers began coinciding through all of the applications.

I've just reviewed Word in Office 2003. Like Office 97, I believe many people will stick with Office 2000 or 2002/XP for quite some time.

Introduction

I am of the opinion that some of the features introduced with Office 2002/XP are a waste of time; there are many other features they could have provided. I don't like the Task Panes or the Smart Tags, they just fill up my work area, and I want the old Mail Merge Wizard back!

I personally run Office 97 SR-1, Office 2000 SR-1, and Office 2002/XP. I've just installed the Office 2003 beta so I could give you some insight into its new features. I'm afraid there's nothing great as far as word processors and desktop publishers go.

In general, I prefer to use the Office 2000 applications for my own work. I prefer it so much that I'm flipping back and forth between Word 2000 and Word 2002/XP to take screen shots of the dialogs as they appear in 2002/XP, and double-checking all of the menu and toolbar options.

Word 2003 brings in XML and expands on a few other features that most of us hard-core Word users may never use.

There, I've finally had my say in front of lots of people. Fair enough.

I'll admit that I like Windows XP Pro's performance over any other prior version, but why-oh-why can't I get it to keep my folder settings? I've set my view to Classic Windows, and every one or two months, I've got the XP style again. What gives?

Ok. I'm done venting.

Introduction

Unless you are a fairly new Word user, I don't suggest you read this book from beginning to end. I certainly did not write it that way. Instead, browse through the Table of Contents and/or Table of Tips and start using some of the information immediately!

Please enjoy. I hope you learn at least one very cool thing from this book, or avoid making one fatal mistake. That ought to be enough to make it pay for itself.

I invite you to email me with any and all comments about this book. I will do my best to answer each and every email.

WordBook@TheOfficeExperts.com

Introduction

This page intentionally left blank.

2. What's New in Word 2003?

Not a whole lot, I'm afraid. They haven't made a better Mail Merge Wizard or gone back to the old one as I'd hoped.

I don't expect to use most of the new features, and don't suppose that most of you reading this book will either. Microsoft seems to think that we all want to do each other's jobs with every program. So, why don't they just make one big program that does everything?

Multiple Versions

I'm hoping it's just an issue with the Beta version…

I have multiple versions of Office running, from 97 to this new beta. When I launch 97 or 2000, it really takes no time at all for the application to open. When launching 2002/XP, it's always taken several moments. When I launch Word 2003 beta, it takes nearly 30 seconds to launch and there is no indication that it is opening; no splash screen or anything until that 30 seconds is up. I am unsure whether this delay occurs on a PC that runs only Office 2003.

Permissions

Just to the right of the Save diskette toolbar icon, there's a button that looks just like European "Do Not Enter" street signs:

This particular symbol means there are no restrictions on the access permissions of this document. To use it, however, you have to install certain other software called "Rights Management" by Microsoft. With this feature, you can set expiration dates on documents, disallow forwarding, and other security features.

Format →Background

Some of you will be disappointed to find that using a background still only works when you save your file as a web page or HTML.

Styles Formatting

We still can't update our styles the easy way, like we could in Word 2000 and below.

Getting Help on the Web

In Word 2000, you could hit Tools→Tools on the Web. Now, it's under Help→Office at Microsoft.com. This takes you to a web full of online Office resources, including consulting services like The Office Experts.

Smart Tags

Now customizable.

Extensible Markup Language (XML)

Save your documents in XML format.

Dictionaries and Thesauruses

Finally, something we may be able to use: the ability to link directly to these resources—online!

Reading Layout

Every time I try to view my book in Reading Layout in Word 2003, it changes my page size to letter size from its current 6" x 9" size. It also took some time for the document to repaginate, which takes no time at all when I switch from Normal to Print Layout view in Word 2000. Seems the more features they add, the slower the program responds.

3. Word's Application Window

In this chapter, I discuss Word's application window and how to navigate through Word while you use it.

Word's application window is similar to that of most Windows programs. Refer to Figure 3-1.

Menus and Toolbars

Understanding the menus and toolbars in Word, how they work and the choices they contain, is crucial for learning Word completely.

Default Menu, Toolbar and Keyboard Settings

Before I begin discussing how-tos and problems, let's set your Word up to keep it from interfering with what you want to accomplish.

The toolbars in Word 2000 are, by default, displayed on one line. Also by default, the menus show only the most recently used commands. I don't want you to read instructions in this book and not be able to find your menu items or toolbars because they're not set to be visible.

Word's Application Window

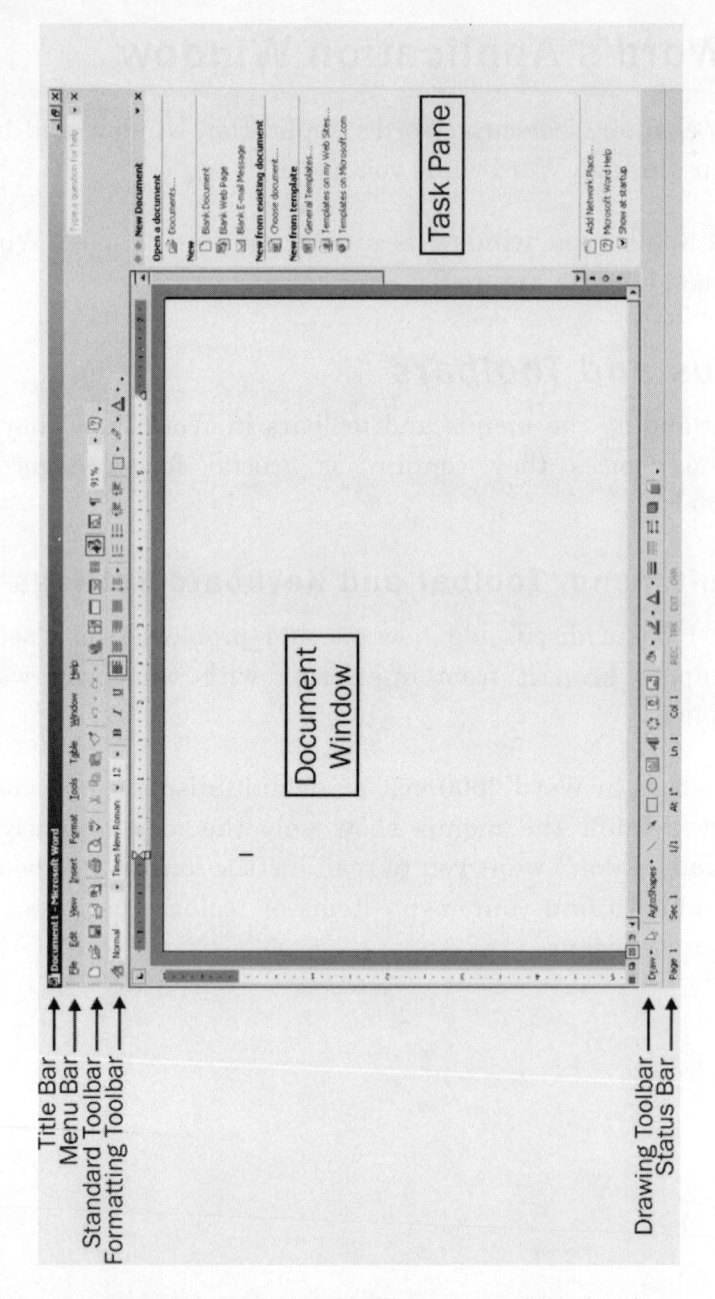

Figure 3-1: Word 2002/XP's Application Window

To change both of these settings at the same time, go to Tools→ Customize and hit the Options tab. Uncheck the top two checkboxes. That's it!

In Office 2002/XP, it's a little bit different. In Word 2002/XP, you will want to have both options checked.

Learn Word's Menus Quickly

Figure 3-2 shows Word's Menu Bar. Note the slightly darker vertical gray bar to the left of the File menu. Clicking and dragging it is a method you can use to move toolbars around in your application window.

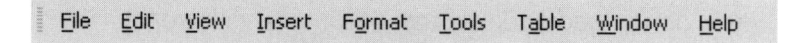

Figure 3-2: Word's Menu Bar

Knowing that a program has a feature or capability is half the battle of truly learning an application. If you're a new Word user and want to learn quickly, you can perform the simple exercise described in the Tip on the next page.

Tip 1: Learn Word's Menus Quickly

Create a list of each of the Menu Bar items and their options. Then, describe each of the choices in your own words. You might be able to describe a lot of them from experience with other applications or just from common sense.

If you don't know what a menu item does, then find out. If you use Word a lot, you may find that you did not know about features you'd been wishing were available!

You don't need to keep the document you create. The intent of the exercise is to make you aware of most of the features available in Word. I find that by writing or typing something, I remember it more easily.

Learn Word's Toolbars Quickly

Word shows the Standard toolbar and the Formatting toolbar by default. I dragged them down into my document window, resized them and then captured them with SnagIt so that I could easily show the entire toolbar at once. When I was done capturing, I simply double-clicked each of their title bars to have them automatically replace themselves where they belong—at the top of my document window.

Refer to Figure 3-3 and Figure 3-4 on the following page.

Word's Application Window

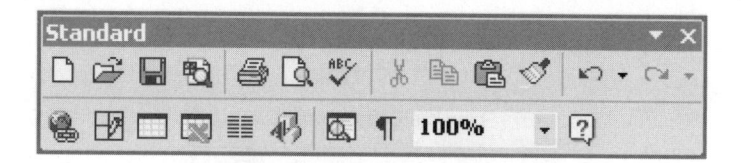

Figure 3-3: Word 2002/XP's Standard Toolbar

Figure 3-4: Word 2002/XP's Formatting Toolbar

If you're a new Word user and want to learn quickly, you can perform these simple steps:

Tip 2: Learn Word's Toolbars Quickly

The purpose of many toolbar buttons can be found simply by hovering the mouse pointer over top of it and reading the Tool Tip. Under Word's Help menu is an option called What's This? See Figure 3-5 on the following page.

Word's Application Window

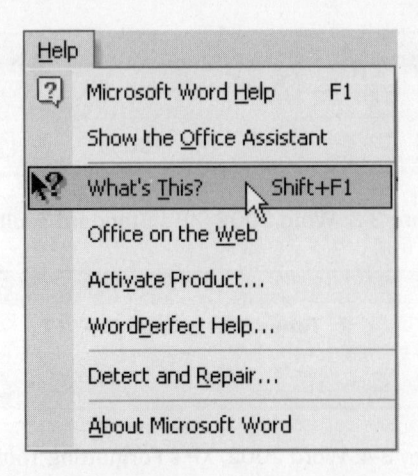

Figure 3-5: Choose "What's This?"

You can also access this option by using the keyboard shortcut Shift+F1. Once you have invoked the What's This? tool, left-click on any toolbar button to learn its purpose. See Figure 3-6 below.

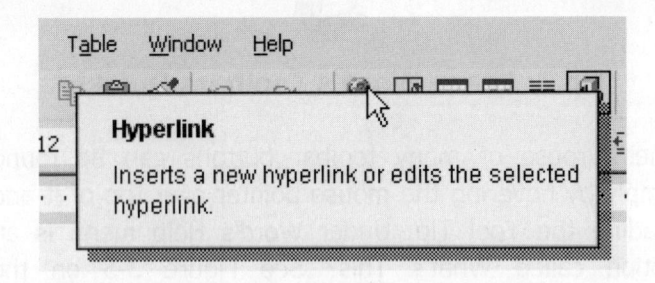

Figure 3-6: Display of the "What's This?" Feature

Word's Application Window

Customizing Menus, Toolbars and Shortcut Settings

Depending on the types of documents you'll be creating in Word, you may want to customize your menus and toolbars to provide quick access to the features you use the most. Menus are much less likely to be customized, so I won't describe that process specifically, as it is very similar to customizing toolbars.

The Commands tab of Word's Customize dialog box is shown in Figure 3-7.

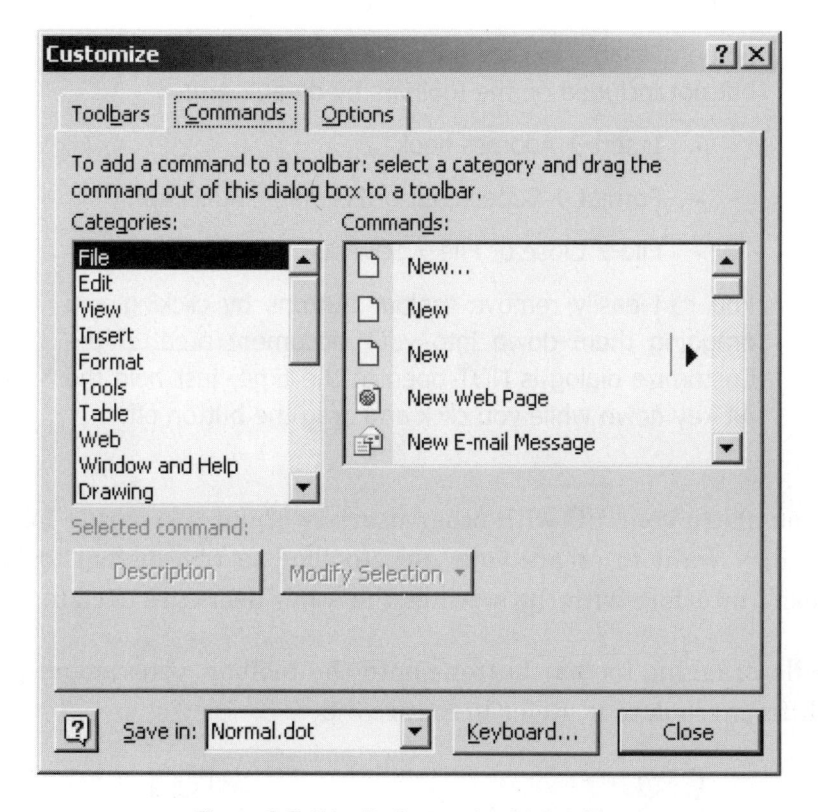

Figure 3-7: Word's Customize Dialog Box

Dreamboat On Word 3-7

Tip 3: Customize Your Toolbars

Using Word's menu, select Tools→Customize. Choose the Commands tab. Click on one Category item at a time and thoroughly review the toolbar buttons available for that category, which are shown in the right-hand column. If you see a toolbar button you might often use, click and drag it directly out of the dialog box and up onto one of your existing Word toolbars.

Some available toolbar buttons that are commonly used, but not included on the toolbars by default are:

> Insert→ Address book

> Format→ Superscript or Format→ Subscript

> File→ Close or File→ Save as

You can easily remove toolbar buttons by clicking and dragging them down into your document area. If the Customize dialog is NOT open at the time, just hold the Alt key down while you click and drag the button off.

If you share your PC with other users (without a separate login), you may want to create your own toolbar so the custom toolbar doesn't interfere with the settings the other users are used to.

While dragging toolbar buttons onto the toolbar, your mouse gets a different look to it. Refer to Figure 3-8.

Figure 3-8: Mouse Buttons

The left-hand graphic depicts what the mouse button looks like while you're dragging a toolbar button or menu item. The **x** indicates that you cannot successfully drop the button or menu item at this location. Once you have your toolbar button or menu item positioned in a location where you can drop it, the **+** sign appears instead.

Customize/Modify Toolbar Buttons

These are the settings you'll find when you assign buttons to toolbars. You can then customize or modify them as follows by choosing the Modify Selection button from the Customize dialog box shown in Figure 3-7.

Name
Type in the name of the button as it should appear on your toolbar if you are going to use the text style button (described below).

Reset Button Image
Select this only if you have begun to edit an existing button image and you would like to reset it to the default.

Edit Button Image
Select this option to "draw" your own button image.

Change Button Image
Select this option to change the existing button image to one of your choosing from Office's collection of button images.

Default Style
Click this button to make the button on the toolbar show just the icon and no text.

Text Only (always)
Click this button to make the button on the toolbar show just the text as it is shown in the Name box, which you can change.

Image and Text
Click this button to make the button on the toolbar show both the icon and the text.

Copy and Paste Image Buttons
Play with these settings to see how you can copy one toolbar button image and put it onto any toolbar button you like.

Resetting Menus and Toolbars
Strangely enough, people lose toolbar buttons and menu bars, and even all of their toolbars from time to time. Please see the Troubleshooting section on page 24-1 to learn how to reset your toolbars back to Word's defaults.

What's With The Taskbar?

When Microsoft came out with Office 2000, everyone screamed and howled about the multiple buttons that appeared on the Windows taskbar. Now, each document that you open in Word gets its own taskbar button. Personally, I like the feature because I use Word much more than other programs, but I can see the argument for others.

The strange thing about this "windows in taskbar" thing is that they made a setting to turn it off in Excel, but not in Word. What's up with that? The only alternative was some lame template that made things even worse. No offense to the coder of that template—I imagine they did their best.

With Word 2002/XP, they finally added the option to turn the feature off. Just go to Tools→Options, View tab and untick the option. If you're using Word 2000, I suggest you just get used to it until you install 2002/XP or above.

Shortcut Keys

Shortcut keys are terrific for people who are more comfortable with the keyboard than with a mouse. Having keyboard references available is also helpful when you're working with important files and suddenly lose the connection to your mouse.

Windows Shortcut Keys

There are few variances between the tasks from one application to the next using the Windows shortcut keys. In Appendix A—Table 1: Windows Keyboard Shortcuts, I list the action that is performed with each of the Windows shortcut keys when used in Word.

Tip 4: Work without your Mouse

The next time you are going to exit Word and shut down your PC, try using these shortcuts instead of your mouse.

First, close all other programs and keep Word open, and then press the following key combinations:

> **Alt** (Accesses Word's menu bar)
>
> **F** (Selects the File menu)
>
> **C** (Closes the current file)
> You may need to perform Alt→ F→ C several times to close all documents. You may need to hit Y or N to save or not save a particular file.

> **Alt** (Accesses Word's menu bar)
>
> **F** (Selects the File menu)
>
> **X** (Exits the application, in this case, Word.)

> **Ctrl+Esc** (Accesses the Windows Start Menu)

> **U** (Invokes shut down menu)
> Choose Shut Down or Turn Off Computer, depending on which version of Windows you're using.

Word Shortcut Keys

I would be irresponsibly wasting trees if I attempted to list all of Word's shortcut keys in this book. Instead, you can make a print out of your own if you want them.

Tip 5: Print a Complete List of Word's Shortcut Keys

To print a list of keyboard shortcuts that have been assigned by you or by someone else that used your PC, simply go to File→ Print and from the Print What dropdown, choose Key Assignments.

My Favorite Shortcut Keys

Some shortcut keys are just okay and others are great. Here are my favorites:

Key	Performs this action in Word:
F4	Repeats the last command. If you are right-handed, you can become very efficient at using your right hand to make selections, and your left hand to hit the F4 key. Use this to quickly apply a style to many paragraphs. Apply a style or a single format to some text normally, using menus or toolbar buttons. Select the next item or just click in the next paragraph you want a style applied to, and hit F4.
Ctrl+Home Ctrl+End	Quickly move to the beginning (Home) or the end (End) of your document using one of these shortcut keys.
Ctrl+Alt+U	Immediately removes all borders of a table. Your insertion point must be inside the table prior to using this shortcut for it to work.
Ctrl+A F9	Use both of these shortcut keys to update the fields in your document. For instance, if you want your Page X of Y numbering to appear properly, the fields must be updated. You can force an immediate update of fields using these keys. Your Table of Contents, if you have one, also updates.

Some other shortcut keys that are great, but aren't Word-specific:

Key	Performs this action:
Ctrl+K	Name completion in Outlook. In the TO box, begin typing the unique part of someone's name. For instance, type Quig for someone whose last name is Quigley. Then hit Ctrl+K. If only one person in your contacts has this four-letter string in their name, then Quigley's name appears in the TO box.
Ctrl+Esc	This brings up the Windows Start menu. Works great if you lose your Windows Taskbar or your mouse operations.
Windows+E	Opens Windows Explorer. The Windows key is the one with the Windows symbol on it:
Print Screen	Use it to take a screenshot. Many people seem unaware that hitting this button sends the screenshot to the clipboard. You can then paste it from there into a Word document or other file.
Alt+Print Screen	This takes a screen shot of just the active window. Works great when making manuals for a software program. Remember, however, that SnagIt from www.Techsmith.com creates much nicer images and provides far more output options.

Windows Dialog Boxes

In any Windows or application dialog box, there are generally buttons like OK, Cancel, Yes, No, etc. The button that is highlighted is the action that is performed when you hit Enter. I've seen many people pick up their mouse to hit OK, when they could just as easily keep their hands on the keyboard and hit Enter.

Referring to Figure 3-9, note that the Yes button is already highlighted, so the user would only need to hit Enter to choose Yes.

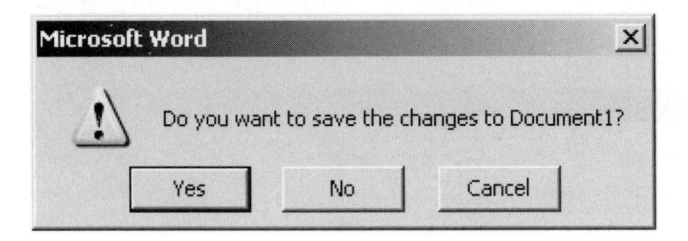

Figure 3-9: Common Word Dialog Box

Many Word users are also proficient typists. We don't want to have to stop typing to pick up the mouse, and we don't have to.

You can navigate through the button choices by using your Tab key. When the desired button is highlighted, hit Enter.

Word's Application Window

Option Settings

The way Word behaves and your screen appears is controlled almost completely by the Tools→ Options menu in Word. Refer to Figure 3-10.

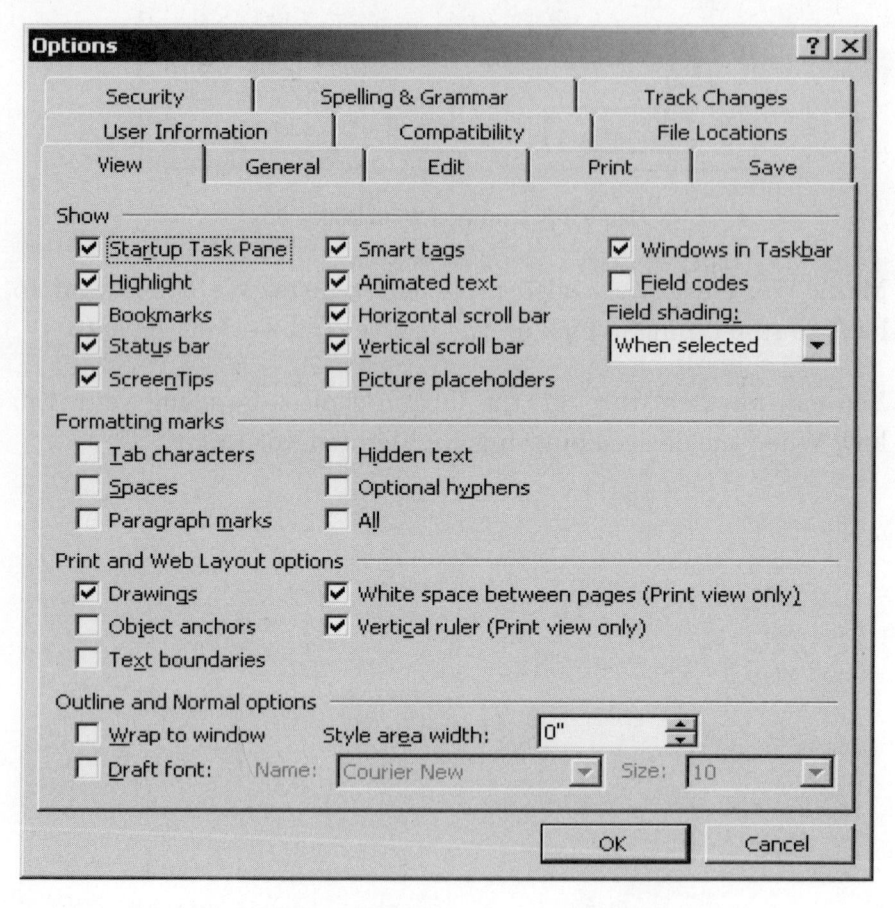

Figure 3-10: Word 2002/XP's Tools→Options Dialog

In Recommended Settings in Word on page A-3, I provide information on the options available in the Options dialog, as well as some comments that may help you to understand Word's options better.

3-16   Dreamboat On Word

AutoCorrect Settings

Microsoft keeps forcing beginners, again and again, to use the features provided by the software. Unfortunately, if you don't know what's happening, it makes Word so much harder to use.

I recommend these settings under Tools→ Autocorrect, Autoformat As You Type: Remove the checkboxes from the top and bottom sections; leave the middle section alone, unless you already know what you want to do differently.

In Word 2002/XP, the Autoformat As You Type tab is different. In this case, remove the options from the 2nd and 3rd sections, leaving the top section alone or setting them as desired.

Just some examples of what you can avoid by using the new settings:

➢ Typing a few underscore characters and hitting Enter, only to have those few characters turn into a border you don't know how to remove. See Other Borders on page 11-3 for instructions to remove unwanted borders.

➢ Having styles automatically created for you. Perhaps you don't intend to use your document as a manual now, but you might want to later. When you really want to use styles in your documents, the ones that have automatically been applied are going to interfere.

➢ If you enter a number in the beginning of a line, type your text and hit Enter, your number is suddenly changed to auto-number formatting.

Word's Application Window

This page intentionally left blank.

4. Features I Love

I would have called this "Features I Like and Sometimes Love," but it would have sounded stupid. Some of these features, like a good medicine, come with bad side effects. But like most doctors, I prescribe these features because of their side effects. The Document Map is a good case in point.

Document Map

While I don't care for the Document Map in theory—it takes up too much room on most monitors—I have used it extensively while creating this document.

Because I am often inserting cross-references to locations I don't remember, I just flip on the Document Map and find it. When I add something new to a section, I may want to go back to some other section and insert a cross-reference to the newly written area.

If you're creating a reference document or even a Help file, you can force the showing of the Document Map by using some VBA code. This would allow users of your document to click on any topic in the Document Map window.

The Document Map is great for these purposes.

Organizer

I wish Microsoft had put the Organizer somewhere more accessible so that it was a better-known feature. Accessing the Organizer must be done by clicking the Organizer button in a dialog box that comes up by choosing one of the following menu options:

- Format→Style
- Tools→Templates and Add-Ins
- Tools→Macro→Macros

The Organizer allows you to copy unseen items, such as Styles, AutoText entries, Toolbars, and Macros, from one document or template to another.

The Organizer dialog is shown in Figure 4-1.

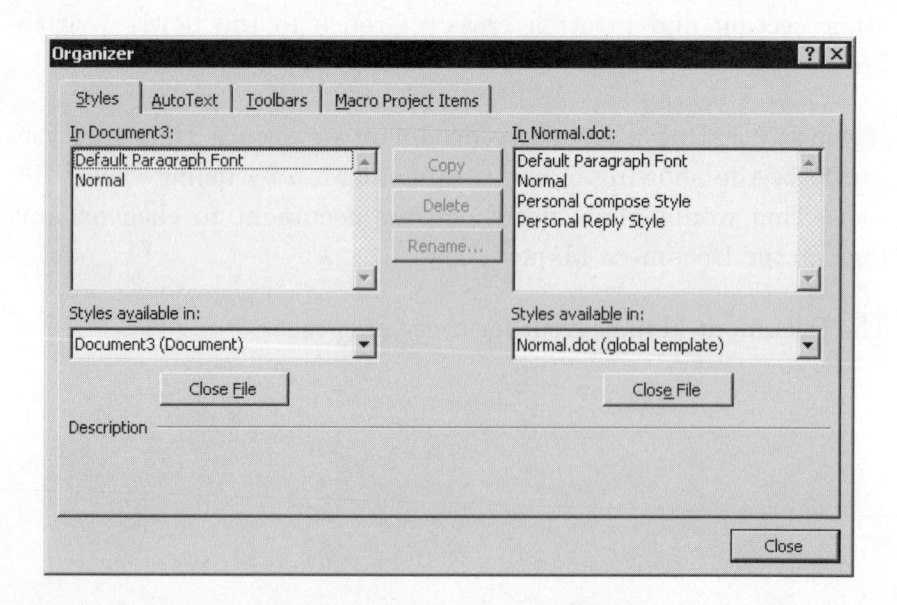

Figure 4-1: The Organizer

You cannot copy AutoText to a Document. AutoText entries are only stored in templates, as shown in the following table.

Item	Copy to Document	Copy to Template
Styles	Yes	Yes
AutoText	No	Yes
Toolbars	Yes	Yes
Macros	Yes	Yes

AutoText

This is a terrific tool that is grossly underused. How often do we find ourselves typing the same things over and over? I used to have a boss who, at the end of every dictated proposal, wanted this line:

"We hope you will find this proposal to be informative and complete. If you have any questions, please don't hesitate to call blah, blah, blah."

Back then, on a Wang word processor, we had to type it each time. Now, with Word's AutoText feature, you can simply create an AutoText entry the first time you type it. Here's how:

Features I Love

Tip 6: Create an AutoText Entry

Select the text that you never want to have to type again. You can include graphics, paragraph returns, tables (but not empty tables!) and just about anything else. When selecting the text, remember to copy any paragraph returns that follow the text so you don't have to type them each time.

From the menu, hit Insert→ AutoText→ New.

Type a simple acronym or other code as a nickname (this is really called an AutoText Name) for this AutoText entry. For best results, try to make it only 4 or 5 letters long. Don't use uppercase letters because they're harder to type. For our example, I might choose "wehope" or perhaps "closeprop" as the name for that AutoText entry. Do NOT use a nickname that otherwise spells a word.

From now on, when you type that nickname and hit Enter, your paragraph is automatically inserted into the document and is already formatted.

Purpose of AutoText Entries

Using AutoText entries is like having a perpetual clipboard always at hand. Try using AutoText entries for the following purposes:

> Letter closings. Include graphic signatures; make one for each of your bosses and name them "sign" followed by their initials, such as "signatp."

- Letterheads that are seldom used. Include your company logo. (You'll be using templates for a letterhead that is often used, right?)

- Your company name. Tired of typing "Amalgamated Properties and Consultants, Inc."? Make an AutoText entry and name it "apci."

- I recently answered a question on the Internet. A VBA coder was trying to figure out where he could store a copy of some text he wanted to insert with a macro button. I told him to have the code run the AutoText entry instead. This worked great for him.

Naming AutoText Entries

If you use less than four letters as your AutoText name, you'll have to enter the three letters and hit the F3 key to activate the AutoText feature. If you use four or more letters, you need only hit Enter after you type the AutoText name.

Use caution when naming your AutoText. If you work for John Allen Randolph, and create an entry named "jar", you may end up with your "Hands caught in the cookie John Allen Randolph"! If you're a fast typist like I am, you won't even see it happen in your document. How embarrassing!

Sharing AutoText Entries

AutoText entries are stored in templates. Either share the template by copying it and giving it to another user/PC or, if they only want the AutoText entries, give them your template and have them use the Organizer to copy the entries into their own templates.

See how to use the Organizer on page 4-2.

Find and Replace

This feature is horribly underused. It's a great tool for everyone. Most of us know how to use it, but how many of us have hit the More and Special buttons?

Hit Ctrl+H to bring up the Find/Replace dialog.

Tip 7: Don't Under-Use Find & Replace

Depending on what you're cleaning up, the order in which you do the finds/replaces can help you work out a great method. If you're constantly cleaning up similar files, you can record your find and replace steps as a macro.

Here are just a few things that make the Find and Replace feature far more useful than many have thought.

As you read, note that the characters such as ^l and ^t are codes that can be found by choosing them under the More→Special buttons. After you use them a time or two, you'll find yourself remembering them.

> You received an email and you'd like to put it into a document. The text comes out all weird and it doesn't wrap.
> 1. First, paste your text by using Edit→ Paste Special, as Unformatted text.
> 2. Hit Ctrl+H.
> 3. Type ^l (that's a carat—above the 6 key, followed by a lower-case L) into the Find What box.
> 4. In the Replace With box, type a space.

5. Hit Replace All. Pasted email text generally uses line breaks instead of paragraph markers as line returns.
6. You'll see the difference when you turn your Show/Hide button on; a line break character looks like this: ↵

➢ Be creative. Do you constantly find too many spaces between words while writing or formatting?
1. Hit Ctrl+H.
2. Type two spaces into the Find What box.
3. In the Replace With box, type a single space. Hit Replace All.
4. Continue to hit Replace All until zero replacements are made. If you like the "two spaces after a colon" format, then follow up by finding a colon and a space, and replacing it with a colon and two spaces.

➢ Someone gave you a document that has two columns of tabbed data. Now, you need to add some items to the lists, but you prefer to use tables. You know that to easily convert this list into a table, you need only one tab between the items in the columns (see Turning Tabbed Columns into a Data File on page 8-4), but the writer places two or three tabs because they used the default tabs instead of setting it up properly.
1. Select the entire list.
2. Hit Ctrl+H.
3. In the Find What box, type ^t^t (this denotes two tab characters).
4. In the Replace With box, type ^t (one tab character).

Features I Love

5. Hit Replace All continuously until zero replacements are made.

➢ You've got a document that uses styles. But you've found it needs to use the styles from another document. You use the Organizer to copy the styles into your document. But how can you easily replace the Heading1 style you used with the H1 style that was used by the other formatter?

1. Hit Ctrl+H.
2. Hit the More button.
3. Hit Format then Style.
4. Hit the letter H to go to the beginning of the styles that start with that letter and choose Heading1.
5. Click in the Replace With box, select Format then Style.
6. Hit the letter H again and choose the style named H1. Don't type anything in the Find What or Replace With boxes.
7. Hit Replace All.

This is a simple way to add an additional heading style as well. You may find that your document is to be one of many and you're asked to change your heading styles to be one level lower than they are now. So, you replace Heading 4 with Heading 5, Heading 3 with Heading 4, Heading 2 with Heading 3 and then Heading 1 with Heading 2.

Notice the order in which they're replaced. Again, the order of your finds and replaces can be very important, while allowing you to be very creative with the tool.

Features I Love

Microsoft Equation

I have known and used the Equation Editor for years, so you can imagine my surprise when I find Word users that aren't even aware that it exists.

When you cannot find the symbol you want using the Insert→Symbol dialog, try the Equation Editor. You can almost always manage to create your own symbol.

I recently got a call from a user who needed the letter "s" with a flat line above it; similar to the line we use to designate a long vowel sound. We were unable to find such a symbol under the Insert→ Symbol dialog.

We went to the Equation Editor using Insert→Object, and choose MS Equation Editor. Figure 4-2 shows what the toolbar looks like.

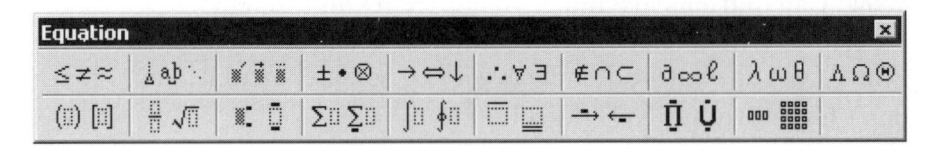

Figure 4-2: Microsoft Equation 3.0 Toolbar

You'll note that you can do all kinds of things with Equation. We chose the 6th box on the bottom row and were able to make the desired symbol: s̄

Dreamboat On Word

Features I Love

You may need to play with the font formatting and other settings, but just a few of the objects you can create using Equation are as follows:

Description	Sample Image
Math problems	$\frac{5}{)5,555}$
Fractions in a different format	$\frac{1}{2}$
Other algebraic and scientific symbols	$\Sigma \div \eta$

Calculations

Wow! Calculations are much easier than you thought!

What's the fastest and easiest way to set up calculations? Please don't forget, this is NOT Excel!

Down and dirty:

1. Create a table.
2. Put the values you want to total in a column.
3. In the last row and the same column, choose Insert→Field, then Equations and Formulas.
4. In the Description box, type: **=Sum(Above)**

Yes, it's that simple. When you create a table, Word sees that table much like Excel sees its cells. I made the following table, inserted the formula as previously described, and you can see how easily it works.

A1	B1	10
A2	B2	20
A3	B3	30
		60

Creating invoices in Word can be so simple using calculations. If your invoices have more than several items, however, you might want to consider using Excel, which can make a very nice document as well, without worrying so much about your table format.

It seems that Word has difficulty keeping track of its cell references, particularly if you merge cells, insert rows and columns, or delete rows and columns.

Format Painter

It's a crime how few people know how to use this feature. It's so great! You receive a document and you love the formatting. But you add a paragraph or two and cannot figure out how the previous author got the paragraphs formatted so nicely when yours look like dirt. Use the Format Painter!

Simply select an original paragraph—the entire paragraph please, including the paragraph return at the end of it—and hit the Format Painter button once. Now click anywhere inside of the paragraph to which you want to apply the same formatting.

If you'd like to apply a certain style throughout your document, like Heading 1, select a paragraph using Heading 1, hit the Format Painter button TWICE (this turns the Format Painter on until you click it again to turn it off) and click once in each paragraph to which you want the Heading 1 style applied.

While the Format Painter cannot fix everything, it can fix your numbered lists and bullets that will not behave. See how in Bullets and Numbering on page 10-1.

Outline View

So underused! While creating this document, I moved the chapters around quite a bit until I felt they were in some logical sequence. Do you think I cut and pasted pages and pages of text? Of course I didn't. I hit View→ Outline view. I clicked on the 1 on the Outline view toolbar so that I could easily view only my Heading 1 styles, which are my chapter names, and clicked and dragged them to their new location.

5. Features I Could Live Without

Let's face it. There are some features in Word that just aren't what they could be. Some are old and some are new. While I use only Microsoft software whenever I can help it, virtually all the programs have their drawbacks and idiosyncrasies. I mean no offense to Microsoft or its coders because there must be a reason why their programs behave the way they do, and include or not include features we'd love to see.

Here are a few of the features and idiosyncrasies I could live without:

Master/Subdocuments

Probably one of the most misused and unnecessary features of Word is the Master/Subdocuments feature. I have found that people don't use it because they need to, but tend to use it because it's there or because some book told them about this feature, but didn't include all the drawbacks of the feature.

Unless you completely understand this feature, don't use it. Find other ways to work around the issues you're having.

Beginning with Word 2000, after you've inserted subdocuments, saved and then opened the file later, the subdocuments are not in view, but are only displayed as hyperlinks. You must click on the hyperlinks to open them. No—there is no way to get around it, so Microsoft has managed to make a bad feature even worse.

Tip 8: When to Use Master/Subdocuments

In my opinion, a master/subdocument setup should only be used when the product you're creating will greatly exceed any reasonable file size. These days, that would be greater than 30 or 40MB. Most machines can handle this file size, while just a few years ago they could not.

If you follow the tips about keeping your file sizes to a minimum in the Graphics and Drawing Tips on page 19-3, you'll reduce the likelihood of needing a master/subdocument setup.

Steps to Master/Subdocuments

Follow these steps to properly create a master/ subdocument setup:

1. Create a template that contains all of the styles that will be used throughout all of the documents. You cannot have one "normal" style in your master and another "normal" style in your subs. If you do not use a common template, you'll get into trouble later.

2. If multiple users are involved in the creation of the document, see Workgroup Templates on page 15-3 to ensure that you are providing a proper template structure for multiple users.

3. Create all of your subdocuments. Do not even think of inserting them into a master until they are completely finished. Do not treat your subdocuments as though they belong together. If you start telling Chapter 3 to start numbering at 3, or tell the page numbers to start at 38, you'll

get all messed up. Set all of the documents up as if they are their own document; all should be Chapter 1 or Section 1, etc.

4. I strongly suggest that you name your subdocuments in the manner of 01-MyFirstChapter, 02-SecondPart, just as long as you use the 01, 02, 03 setup. You'll be so glad later, and there's no explanation needed. You'll say, "Ohhhh, I get it!"

5. Create the master. The master, ideally, contains only a cover page and Table of contents (TOC), and perhaps some other non-subject-matter-related information. The master must also use the same template. Of course, the master can be created first if you like, but the following part should be done absolutely last.

6. Now, insert a section break. Go to View→Master (Word 97) or View→Outline view (Word 2000 and above). Hit the Insert Subdocument button and insert your file number 01-MyFirstChapter. Insert each subdocument after that. Save the file.

7. NEVER edit subdocuments through the master. You must edit them by themselves. The only time you should open the master is to edit the master text at the beginning, to update the TOC or to print the file.

8. The file structures must be maintained. So, suppose you've got linked graphics in subdocuments that are in a master and you want to ship the whole kit and kaboodle to Denver. Do the work up front. Create a folder called MyProject or whatever. Under that, structure your files into folders as shown in Figure 5-1:

Features I Could Live Without

```
⊟ 📁 MyProject
    📁 Graphics
    📁 Master
    📁 SubDocuments
```

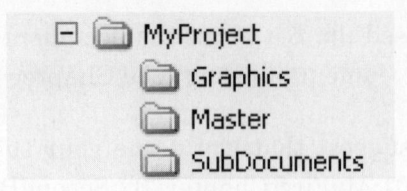

Figure 5-1: Master/Subs File Structure Layout

9. Now, if you don't have graphics to worry about (they are embedded or you have none), then don't make an individual folder for them. The bigger the project/documents are, the more important and helpful the folders can be. If you're in charge of the graphic files too, it sure is nice to have your graphics named 01Graphicname, 02Graphicname, and so on.

Troubleshooting Master/Subdocuments

So...you already did it. You created a Master/ Subdocument layout and now you're unable to properly make changes to the document. "Undo" it this way:

1. Open the master or subdocument that is using most of the styles that you want to use throughout the whole project. Save that file as a template called MyProjectTemplate or whatever—check that your template location is where everyone who needs to can get to it. Delete everything out of it (Ctrl+A and hit the Delete key). Save it, close it.

2. Open your master again. Hit Tools→Templates and Add-ins and attach the new template to your master. Check the box that says automatically update styles. Save it, close it.

3. Open each subdocument by itself and do the same. You'll hate me when some of your styles/formatting change but this will be your own fault because you didn't listen (seriously, this won't happen to you anymore and you can be glad of that!). You may need to clean up some formatting like page numbering, etc.

5-4   Dreamboat On Word

4. If everything is still okay and your document hasn't locked up on you yet, you're way ahead of the game.

Unlocking Master Documents

Corrupt Document? Hardly.

If you're in big trouble and your master document is locked and you can't do much of anything, this isn't because the file is corrupt, it's because you didn't follow the rules, which I've never seen anywhere in their entirety except when I finally posted it as an FAQ on www.Tek-Tips.com.

Why does it occur? This particular problem occurs because the subdocuments were edited via the master document.

Read this whole topic so that you understand the following steps completely:

1. Open the master document. Hit File→Save As and give it a new name. Now it's not a master anymore. Put the new master file into its own folder and make your folder structure as I've described above. Open the original master, save it as a template, delete everything out of it as described above, save it and close it.

2. Open the new master and connect it to the new template as described above.

3. Select all of the pages of the first chapter and hit Cut. Hit File→ New and pick the template. In the new document, hit paste. Save it as 01-MyFirstChapter or similar, and close it. Continue doing this with each chapter until you've got all of the chapters cut and pasted into their own documents with the new naming structure and the new folder structure.

4. At this point, the master should not contain any of the subdocument parts. Save it. Insert a section break at the end of this new master, and then insert your subdocuments as described above. Update the TOC. Save. Close. All done.

AutoFormat

The AutoFormat feature in both Word and Excel tends to unnecessarily bloat file sizes. It never seems to work the way its name implies, except with the simplest documents and spreadsheets. Of course, you should try it out, but I don't recommend counting on it until you've mastered it.

Indexing

Creating indexes is painful. That's all there is to it. Regardless of the pain involved, I see many people using indexes when they're just not necessary. A 100-page document certainly doesn't need an index, particularly if it already has a well-defined table of contents.

Tip 9: Fastest Method to Creating an Index

In my opinion, the easiest way to create an index is by using the concordance file method. Search for the word "concordance" under Word's help for instructions.

You'll likely need the person that determines the index entries to go through a hard copy of the document and highlight—with a highlighter pen—every word that should be indexed. They only have to highlight each word one time. Then, create a concordance file according to Word's Help.

It's still a tedious task even when you use this easier method.

The Web Toolbar

I don't know about you, but I'll still never get used to it. I hate that it pops up every time I'm using a hyperlink. It may be nice if you want to publish your document electronically, but it would be nice to have an option to use it or not.

Default Document View

I hate Normal view. I work only in Page Layout (Word 97) or Print Layout (higher versions) view. I believe we should be able to set our own default view, but the view last used on the document is the view you'll get when you open it. I force Word to bend to my will by using a macro in my normal.dot file. You can find the macro on page 21-16.

Cross-References

As I write this book, I provide cross-references like the one at the end of the previous topic. First, I insert the text for the cross-referenced, numbered item for my Sample Word Macros section. I then want to insert the page number of the same section.

Unfortunately, I have many, many bookmarks in this file, and when I choose to insert the cross-reference for the page number, I need to scroll all the way down to the same location in the cross-reference list. I would like it much better if it stayed on the selection that I last used.

When we create long documents—and let's face it, we rarely use cross-references in short documents—there are going to be many cross-references listed. We're naturally going to be working in the same area of the document for a period of time. So it doesn't make sense that the list pops back to the first item in the list again and again.

Features I Could Live Without

Envelopes and Labels

There are only a few things I don't like, but they've been around forever and confused so many people. And people get confused even more if they aren't aware that they must use the Mail Merge menu features if they want to create mail merged envelopes or labels.

Envelopes

A lot of people have difficulty with the Envelopes because of the way you're asked to load the envelope into the printer. I personally hate it because I can only print the envelope once. I cannot quickly create three or four envelopes.

Tip 10: Fast Envelopes

1. Create a new document.
2. Go to File→Page setup. For the paper size, choose Com10 or business envelope; choose Landscape layout.
3. Choose the paper source (the envelope feed tray or manual feed tray, whichever the case may be).
4. Set the margins approximately as follows or adjust as necessary:
    - Top: 2.25"
    - Bottom: 0.5"
    - Left: 4.25"
    - Right: 0.5"
5. Hit Ctrl+A and change the font as desired. Save the file as a template called envelope.dot and close it.

Now, whenever you want to create an envelope, just hit File→-New and choose the template. You can create many

Features I Could Live Without

by hitting Ctrl+Enter (to insert a page break) after each address is typed.

If you want a return address, you can insert it as a header in the envelope.

Labels

The labels are pretty self-explanatory, but there are a couple of things that confuse people.

First is the fact that if you want a whole sheet of labels into which you can type any address you want, you need to hit the New Document button after you've selected your label type.

Not only that, but if you commonly use a specific label type, you can save this "new document" as a template. Thereafter, you can hit File→New and pick your labels template without having to choose the label type each time, etc.

A very important note: Please be sure you are viewing table gridlines whenever working with labels. To my knowledge, all the label formats are created using tables. If you're not viewing table gridlines, you can easily get lost in the structure of your labels.

To show gridlines in your tables, hit Table→Show Gridlines. It's the last menu option under the Tables menu. If you don't see it, but you do see Hide Gridlines, then you're already viewing table gridlines.

Another thing: Most people have no need to download the Avery wizards. The most common of the product templates are already installed with Word.

Do not bother trying to access these templates by finding a file on your PC—they don't exist. I believe that Word contains programming code to create them on-the-fly.

Dreamboat On Word   5-9

Features I Could Live Without

This page intentionally left blank.

6. Fonts and Formatting

There are many different formatting features in Word. I hope to cover the basics and deal with the problems that can occur with each one. I'll cover them in the same order that they appear under the Format menu in Word.

I cannot say enough about the benefits of having the Show/Hide option turned on to Show when working with formatting. You can use Ctrl+Shift+* as the shortcut key or click the Show/Hide button, which looks like Figure 6-1 and is found on the standard toolbar:

Figure 6-1: Show/Hide Button in ON position (Word XP/2000)

Styles are covered on page 9-1.

Considerations

While it may seem like common sense, I feel the need to mention this anyway.

Suppose you're a new company and creating a layout design for your letterhead. You might love a certain font that you have, or you may even have someone develop a custom font for you. I strongly encourage you to use that font only in graphic images. For the main text in your letterhead and website, choose "safe" fonts.

Fonts and Formatting

Too Many Fonts

Many programs, including Word, don't seem to like it when you have too many fonts installed. I personally recommend less than 500 fonts.

If you have many fonts, place the non-standard ones in another folder called MoreFonts. Then, if you decide you need one, install it via the Control Panel in Windows and by double-clicking on Fonts. Then use the File→Install New Font menu.

> Note: *You cannot install fonts through any of Word's menus.*

Safe Fonts

Microsoft (I believe) came up with a term called "Web-Safe Fonts." These are fonts that virtually everyone has installed on their PC. If you use a non-standard font on your webpage, it will appear differently for people who do not have that font installed. Some very popular web-safe fonts are Times New Roman, Arial, Verdana and Tahoma.

The same goes for Word and any other Microsoft program. If you have installed graphics programs like CorelDraw, you may have installed additional fonts at the same time. After these fonts have been installed, there is no easy way to distinguish which fonts came from Windows and which ones came from CorelDraw.

So you should be very careful to choose fonts that will likely reside on everyone's PC. If you use fonts that you believe are non-standard, then you should use them only in graphics. It will be easier for you to just choose standard fonts.

Font Dialog Box

Ctrl+D brings up the Font dialog box, from which you can format all aspects of the font of the text that is currently selected.

For fancy formatting, check out the effects that are provided under the Text Effects tab of this dialog. I don't recommend using any of those features in a serious document, such as a manual or a proposal to a client.

Tip 11: Set the Default Font for All New Documents

This is a commonly asked question and the answer is simple. Open any document or just a new, blank document. Hit Format→ Font and set your desired font and size. Hit the Default button at the bottom left of the Font dialog.

If you want to make font changes while making other changes to your normal.dot, then you'll need to open normal.dot, hit Ctrl+A and THEN change the font.

Figure 6-2 shows the Font dialog box.

Fonts and Formatting

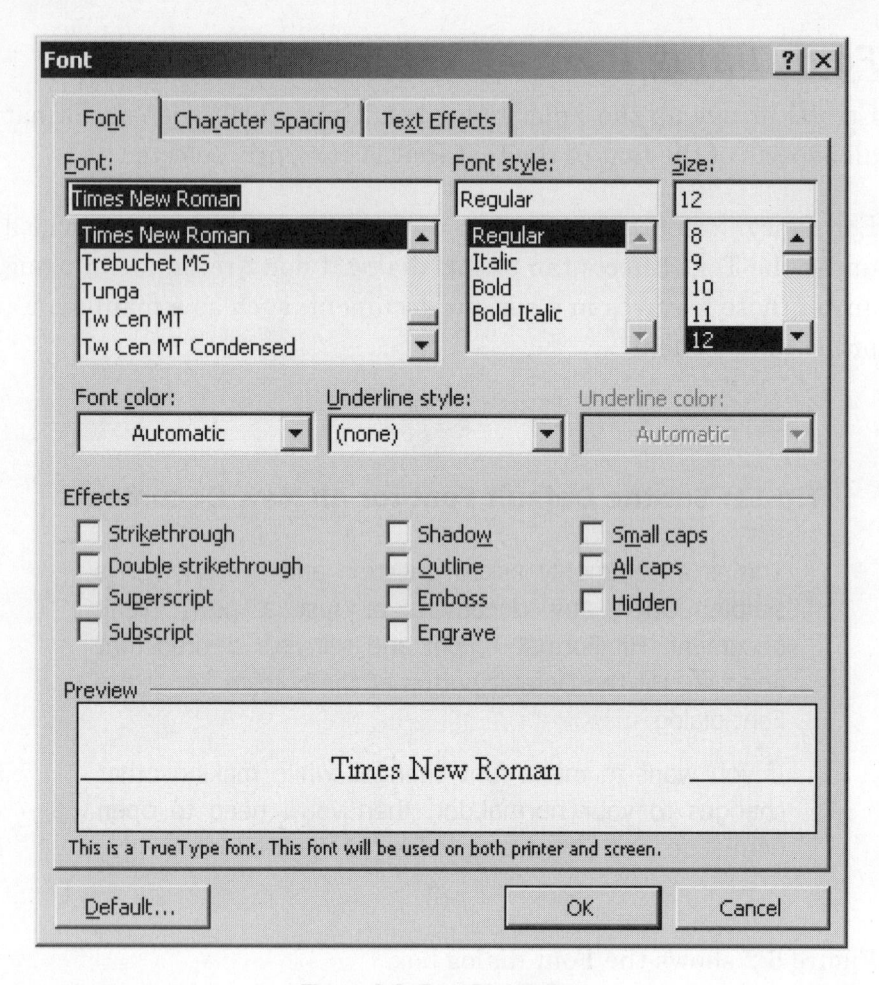

Figure 6-2: Font Dialog Box

Tip 12: Cautions for Using Font Formatting

Hidden Text: Be careful when choosing Hidden as your text format. Showing or hiding text that has been formatted to be hidden is an option on each user's PC. Hidden text is great if you intend to write instructions for persons "in-house," but you won't want to use it for documents that are sent externally.

Unusual Fonts: If you use unusual fonts, you may find that when you send a document to someone else, it will look different. Why? Because that font may not be available on their PC.

Symbols: Watch those symbols and bullets. Be sure you use common fonts for them as well. While it might be a smiley face on your PC, it could turn into an email icon on someone else's.

Avoid WordPerfect Fonts: Many people convert their documents from WordPerfect files that generally use default fonts of Univers and CGTimes. These are not Windows fonts. While they may be installed on your system because you have or once had WordPerfect installed, they may not be on all systems. If you convert WordPerfect files to Word, you'll want to also Ctrl+A and change the fonts to Windows fonts. To my knowledge, the closest to Univers is Arial and the closest to CGTimes is Times New Roman.

For information on Character styles, see the section on Styles on page 9-1.

This page intentionally left blank.

7. Paragraph Formatting

The Format Paragraph dialog is shown in Figure 7-1.

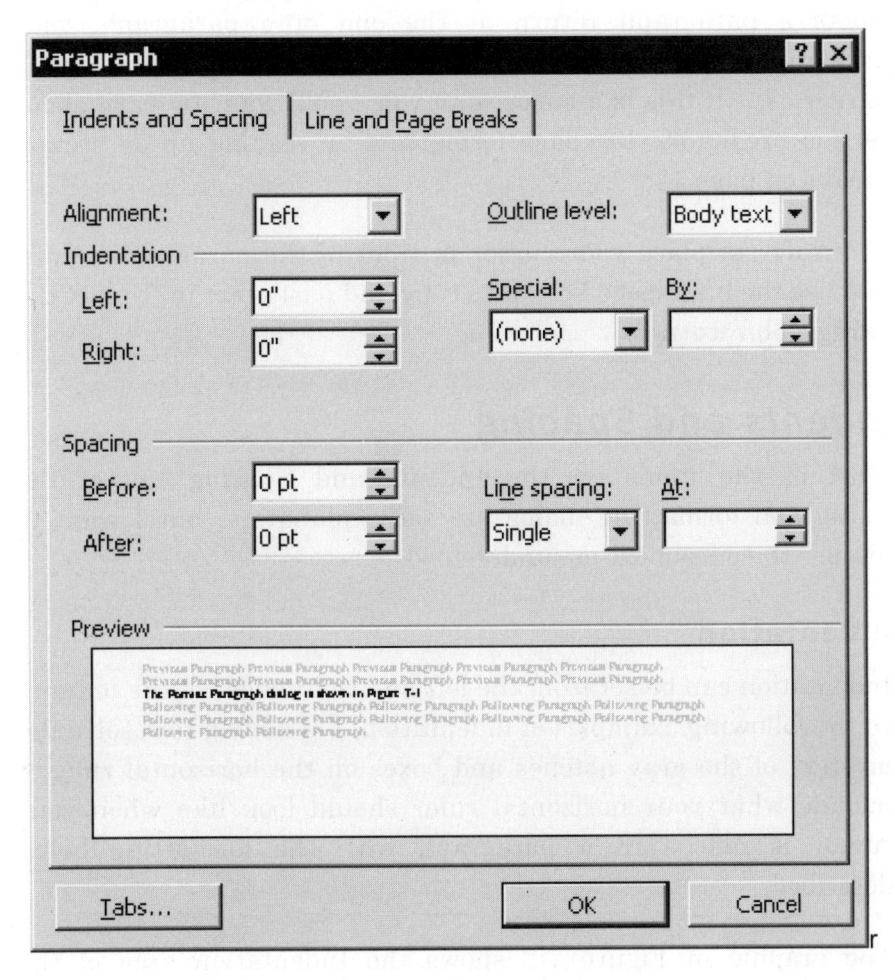

Figure 7-1: Paragraph Formatting Dialog Box

Paragraph Formatting

Here's the big secret about paragraph formatting. People who don't know the secret are baffled by certain behavior in Word.

Paragraph formatting is stored in the paragraph return. If you delete a paragraph return at the end of a paragraph, your paragraph may suddenly take on the formatting of the following paragraph. (If this is a surprise to you, you'll want to learn about section breaks storing page formatting by reading up on section breaks on page 13-1.)

It is safer to place your cursor in front of the paragraph return and use the backspace key, or to copy and paste text in front of the paragraph return.

Indents and Spacing

Most of the items on the Indents and Spacing tab of the Paragraph formatting dialog are self-explanatory, but I want to discuss the ones most misunderstood.

Indentation

Indentation can be set from the left and right edges of the margin. In the following examples of indentation, I'm hoping to resolve the mystery of the gray notches and boxes on the horizontal ruler. I include what your horizontal ruler should look like when your cursor is placed in a paragraph with the formatting being described.

The graphic in Figure 7-2 shows the Indentation area of the Paragraph Formatting dialog box.

Paragraph Formatting

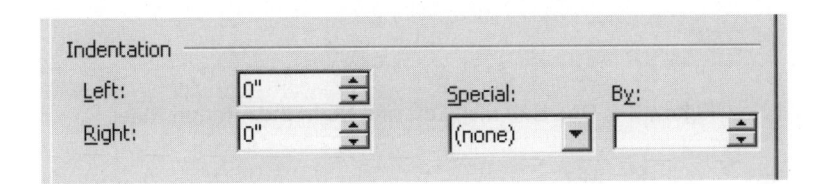

Figure 7-2: Indentation Settings

For a frame of reference, a normal horizontal ruler in a four-inch-wide document with no indentation settings looks like Figure 7-3.

Figure 7-3: Horizontal Ruler with No Indentation Settings

If my right-hand margin is 1-inch, and I indent it 1/2-inch, then my text will print to within 1.5 inches from the right-hand edge of the paper.

> You can offset or emphasize text by using indentation on both sides. This paragraph is formatted with a half-inch indent left and right.

When choosing to set up a single paragraph as above, it is easiest if you type the paragraphs before and after it, and then select only that paragraph before setting the indents. Otherwise, your following paragraph needs to be set back to zero indents. You can save a lot of back-and-forth formatting by formatting your document after all text has been typed, or at least by typing large chunks of text, and then going back to format it before moving on to another chunk.

Having a half-inch indent on both the left- and right-hand sides of the margins results in a horizontal ruler that looks like Figure 7-4. Of course, the document was set to be only four inches wide so that I could fit a reasonable looking ruler onto our page.

Paragraph Formatting

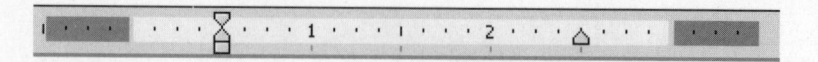

Figure 7-4: One-Half-Inch Left and Right Indentation Ruler

You can reset the indentations to zero by dragging the box under the left hand side over to the left and align it with the dark gray area, and drag the triangle at the right-hand side over to the dark gray area at the right.

Tip 13: Fix Disappearing Table Text

If the text runs off the end of your table into oblivion, check the indentation. I've seen lots of documents where people have somehow inadvertently managed to get a right indent setting. For best results, always use a zero right indent in table text.

Be careful! There can be negative indent settings, too, and these can really make the formatting appear difficult to fix.

Paragraph Formatting

Special Indentation

There are only two options here.

     This paragraph shows a half-inch First Line indent. Years ago, we wrote our letters and many documents using an indent on the text as depicted on this paragraph. It is not nearly so popular as it used to be, nor is it any longer considered more correct over what we called "block style," which is more commonly used today and contains no indent.

The First Line Indent setting makes the horizontal ruler display as shown in Figure 7-5. You can reset it to no indentation by dragging the triangle that hangs from the top of the ruler to align with the one on the bottom-left of the ruler.

Figure 7-5: First Line Indentation Ruler

This paragraph uses a half-inch Hanging indent. Hanging indents are commonly used for bullets, too. As you can see, only the second and sequential lines are indented by the measurement. Using bullets effectively inserts a symbol and a tab. The difference is that a tab stop is placed at the same location as the indent measurement when you set a bullet.

Hanging indents look like Figure 7-6 on the horizontal ruler. You can easily remove it by dragging the square to the left margin, below the triangle on the top of the ruler.

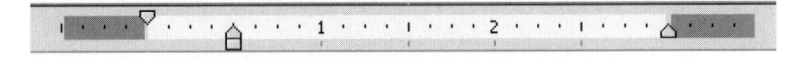

Figure 7-6: Hanging Indentation Ruler

Dreamboat On Word   7-5

Spacing Between Paragraphs

If you want your long documents to be as compact in size as possible, and to use all of the features of Word as they're intended, then stop using paragraph returns to put sufficient space between one line of text and the next.

Tip 14: Spacing between Paragraphs

> Using paragraph returns to provide spacing between paragraphs unnecessarily bloats your document with unseen and unused characters.
>
> Instead, use Space Before and After text.

For instance, the Body text style used in this document is formatted with 0 pts before and 12 pts after each paragraph, and line spacing of at least 15 points.

To change the spacing, first place your cursor somewhere within the paragraph text. Hit Format→ Paragraph.

Space before and after can be changed as shown in Figure 7-7.

```
Spacing
  Before:   6 pt          Line spacing:    At:
  After:    12 pt         Multiple  ▼      1.25
    ☐ Don't add space between paragraphs of the same style
```

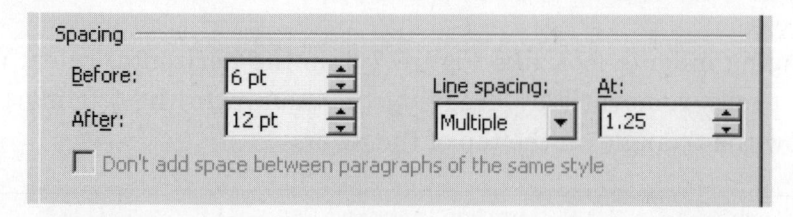

Figure 7-7: Spacing Before and After, and Line Spacing

Tip 15: Using List Boxes in Dialogs

Note the selection arrows in the graphic on the preceding page. There is no need to use only the arrows; you can just as easily click inside of any box like this and type in your entry, then tab to the next box, or hit Enter to close the dialog.

Likewise, most boxes that show incremental measurements, such as points or inches, do not require that you enter that measurement's symbol. Simply type the value you want. I used this method to get the before and after spacing on this document.

Paragraph Formatting

This page intentionally left blank.

8. Tabs

By the time I completed writing the Tabs section, I realized that there was enough material for its own chapter. It doesn't seem like such a tough thing until you try to explain the anomalies to others.

There are six types of tabs in Word. Here, I'll describe each one, display the results of using it, and list some common mistakes made by users.

One of the most common mistakes is to overlook what you have selected when setting a tab. Before setting a tab, be sure you have selected all of the text or paragraphs to which you want the setting to apply.

Tip 16: Using Tables instead of Tabs

There will be many times when it is much easier for you to use a table layout instead of tabs. Review the Tables chapter on page 12-1, learn how best to create tables and use them whenever possible. I found that it had been a long time since I created tabbed lists until I wrote this section on tabs; I almost always use tables. It's much easier to center your column headings and align your information or bulleted lists.

IMPORTANT: To create tabs within table cells, you must hold the Ctrl key while hitting Tab. However, setting the tabs is done in the same manner as creating tabs within paragraphs.

Different tabs can be chosen from the button to the far left of the horizontal ruler, as shown in Figure 8-1. Using this button and the horizontal ruler is the easiest method of setting tabs. Sometimes, you must use the dialog box, which is explained on page 8-10.

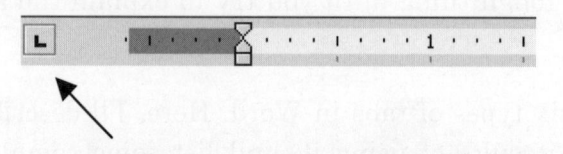

Figure 8-1: Tab Type Selector Tool

Default Tab Settings and Potential Problems

By default, there are 1/2-inch, left-aligned tab settings across the page. Setting any tab manually overrides the default tab settings up to that point from the left of the page. For instance, setting a left-aligned tab at the 3-inch mark effectively "erases" all of the 1/2-inch tabs set by default up to the 3-inch mark. The 1/2-inch default tabs beyond the three-inch mark remain.

Default tabs are barely viewable on the horizontal ruler, which can be confusing. If you look closely, however, you'll see the default tab settings.

Figure 8-2 depicts first the horizontal ruler with default tabs only, then enlarged so that you can see the small, gray tick-mark indicators, and then with a 3-inch, manually set tab.

Tabs

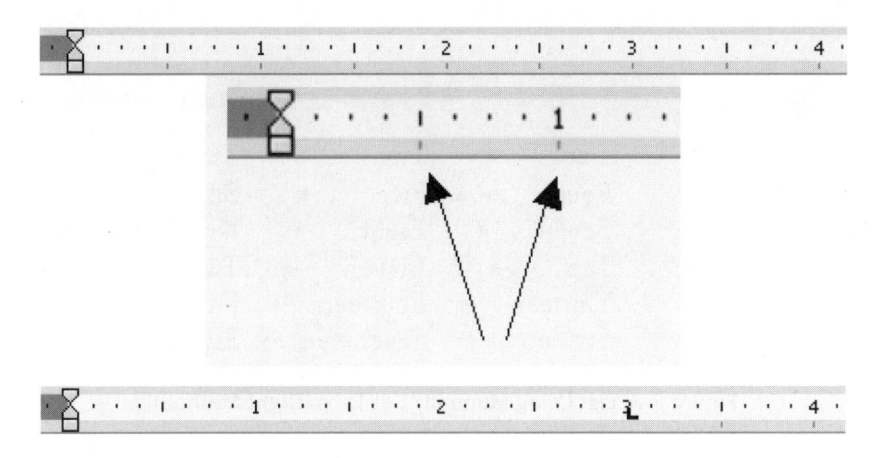

Figure 8-2: Reading Tab Settings on the Horizontal Ruler

As a result of the default tab settings, many users type columns of information, as shown in Figure 8-3. This is not the desired method, which is shown in Figure 8-4.

Note the difference in the number of tabs required. In a large document, you could save considerable file size by the reduction of unnecessary characters (tabs).

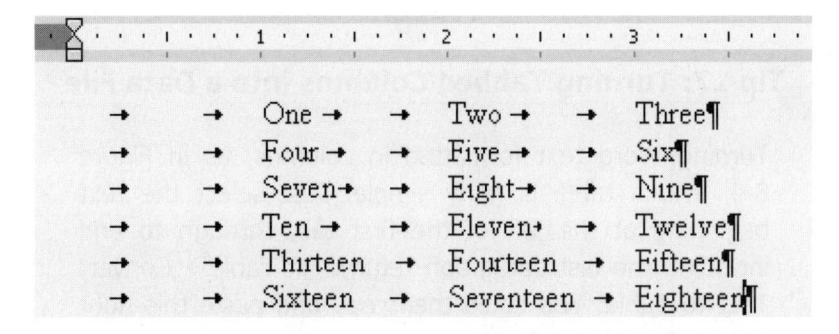

Figure 8-3: List Using Default Tab Settings (Wrong Method)

Dreamboat On Word 8-3

One	Two	Three
Four	Five	Six
Seven	Eight	Nine
Ten	Eleven	Twelve
Thirteen	Fourteen	Fifteen
Sixteen	Seventeen	Eighteen

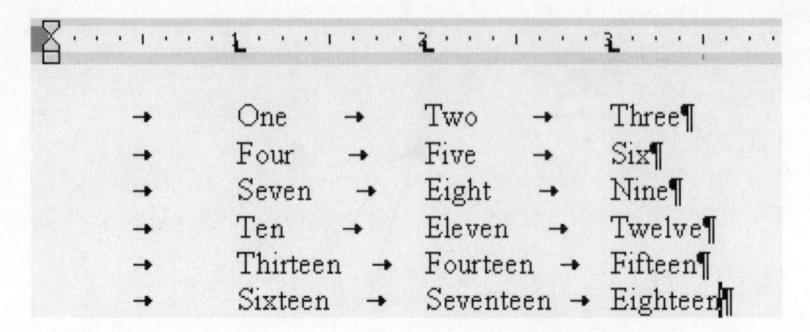

Figure 8-4: List Using Manually Set Tabs (Right Method)

I recently received a file that was about 9 columns wide and 11 pages long, and used the wrong method. The list should probably have been created in Excel in the first place because it was just for reference. Ultimately, we were to get this data into an Access table. Formatting like an Excel workbook or even a Word table would have been great for this purpose. Unfortunately, we could not automate getting the list into the required layout.

Tip 17: Turning Tabbed Columns into a Data File

Turning Word text formatted in columns, as in Figure 8-4, into a table is fairly simple. Just select the text beginning at the left of the first tab, through to and including the last paragraph return. Hit Table→ Convert Text to Table. You could then copy and paste this right into an Excel worksheet.

If your text contains more than one tab between each item, you must first run a Find and Replace from the Edit menu to replace two tabs with one, until zero replacements have been made.

The problem arises when your text extends beyond the left alignment measure of the following tab. So, many people set their list as shown in Figure 8-5. Then, when an attempt is made to convert this data to some other format, it simply does not work.

→	One	→	Two	→	Three¶
→	Four	→	Five	→	Six¶
→	Seven	→	Eight	→	Nine¶
→	Seven	→	Eight	→	Nine¶
→	and·a·half	→	and·a·half	→	and·a·half¶
→	Ten	→	Eleven	→	Twelve¶
→	Thirteen	→	Fourteen	→	Fifteen¶
→	Sixteen	→	Seventeen	→	Eighteen¶

Figure 8-5: List Text That Exceeds the Column Width (Wrong Method)

I have found that the best way to create all types of columned lists is to place them in tables in the first place and then just remove the borders of the table, if desired. Long bulleted lists are best handled this way too.

If you cannot use tables, then type your list using NO tab at the beginning of the line and only one tab between each column. When you've finished typing the list, THEN select it all and set your left indent and appropriate tabs. Depending on the length of text you type in any given column, you may have to change your tab width, so you might as well finish the list before formatting.

Left-Aligned Tab

This is the tab setting most commonly used. To set a left-aligned tab, click on the button at the far left of the horizontal ruler until you see a button that looks like the one in Figure 8-6.

Figure 8-6: Left-Aligned Tab Marker

Then, click where you'd like the first left-aligned tab marker to appear on your horizontal ruler. Left-aligned tab markers are best used for the types of lists previously discussed.

Center-Aligned Tab

Hit View→Header and Footer. You'll see that this tab setting is used by default in Word's headers and footers.

Figure 8-7: Center-Aligned Tab Marker

By default, you can type, for instance: the section name, hit tab, the document title, hit tab, and then "Page" (followed by a space) and insert the page number field. This left-aligns the section name, centers the manual name, and right-aligns the page number on the top of your document, as shown in Figure 8-8.

MySectionName → MyDocumentTitle → Page 1

Figure 8-8: Using Default Header/Footer Tab Settings

There is a center tab marker at the 3-inch mark and a right-aligned tab at the right-hand margin.

Be sure not to use the center-aligned tab when you can just as easily use the center alignment on the paragraph. Using the tab, for instance, would not be appropriate when you simply want to center one item of text on a line.

Right-Aligned Tab

Once again, don't use a right-aligned tab to right-align one item of text. For instance, if you're putting the date at the top-right of your page, just right-align the paragraph instead of creating a right-aligned tab setting.

The right-aligned tab button is depicted in Figure 8-9.

Figure 8-9: Right-Aligned Tab Marker

Use the right-aligned tab setting when you need to type more than one item of text on the line, as shown in Figure 8-10.

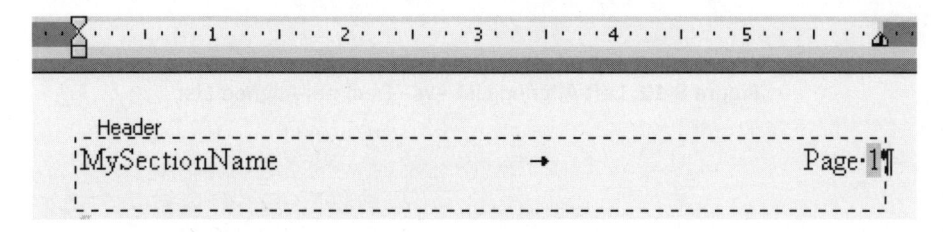

Figure 8-10: Using Right-Aligned Tab Marker Setting in a Header

Tabs

Decimal-Aligned Tab

This tab setting is often misunderstood. The only time you'll really want to use it is for typing columns of measurements. For currency, you can generally just use a right-aligned paragraph format. However, you may have a list of chemical test results that you'd like lined up properly.

Figure 8-11: Decimal-Aligned Tab Marker Button

Figure 8-11 depicts the decimal-aligned tab marker button. I used this setting when creating the list shown in Figure 8-12. Note how it's much easier to see how the numbers relate to each other in value by using the decimal-aligned list at the right of the figure. The vertical line in the graphic is for reference only.

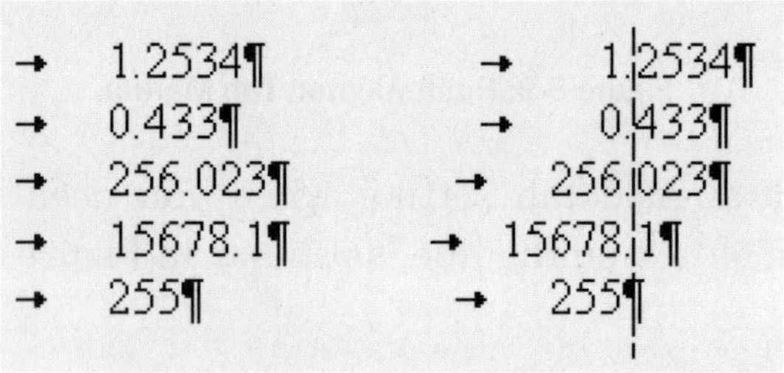

```
→  1.2534¶        →    1.2534¶
→  0.433¶         →    0.433¶
→  256.023¶       →  256.023¶
→  15678.1¶       →  15678.1¶
→  255¶           →    255¶
```

Figure 8-12: Left-Aligned List –vs– Decimal-Aligned List

Bar Tab

Okay, okay...I know what it sounds like, but this one won't cost you any money.

The bar tab marker is shown in Figure 8-13. I've never found a particular purpose for this tab setting. However, there are many Word users who do special things such as legal documents or medical transcription, and it may very well be perfect for some users.

Figure 8-13: Bar Tab Marker Button

Using the bar tab does not appear to do anything more than place a vertical line on the tabbed list, as shown in Figure 8-14.

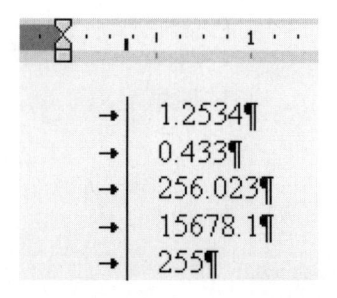

Figure 8-14: List with Bar Tab Setting

Using the Tab Settings Dialog Box

For some tab settings, you must use the dialog box. Choose Format→ Tabs to bring up the dialog. Remember that prior to setting any tabs, you must first select the text to which you would like the tab settings to apply. Having your cursor on the first line of a tabbed list prior to changing a tab setting changes that line only.

Figure 8-15 shows the Tabs dialog box. From it, you can choose the type of alignment and the Leader you want. A tab leader is the character that is used between the first item of text and the second item of text. Generally, there is none.

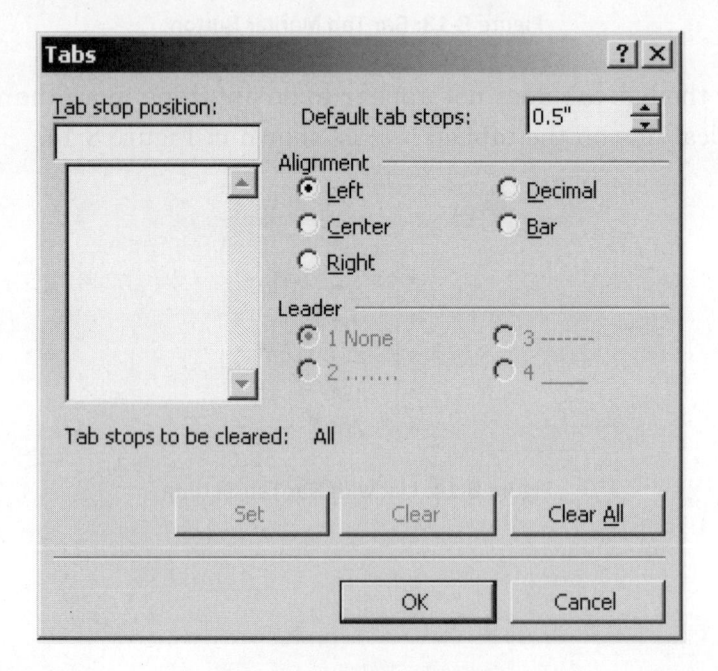

Figure 8-15: Tabs Dialog Box

For best results, on opening the tabs dialog box, hit the Clear All button to clear any previously set tabs before applying your own.

Leaders

A list using a dot leader (Leader #2) with a right alignment is shown in Figure 8-16. You can use this for lists such as the one shown, for menus, tables of contents (though I hope you'll let Word create these for you automatically!) and other reference lists. I don't recommend using leaders that extend far across the page and have very little text. It would be harder to read. If you have long lists, and like using the leaders, I suggest using a column format so that it's not hard to travel your eyes across the leader to the referenced text.

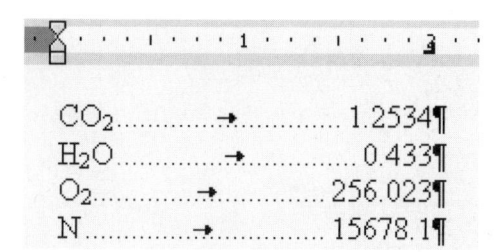

CO_2...→............1.2534¶
H_2O......→............0.433¶
O_2.........→............256.023¶
N.............→............15678.1¶

Figure 8-16: Dot Leader, Right-Aligned Tab Setting

Other leaders work the same as the dot leader. They just use different characters.

This page intentionally left blank.

9. Styles

I've found that most people avoid using styles until they absolutely must. Then, when they finally learn how to use them, they are so upset about not having learned about them before.

If you are creating templates, I'd like you to consider the following before you begin:

Tip 18: Style Hints for New Templates

Just a few things to keep you out of trouble when creating templates for your documents and manuals.

Use "safe" fonts as described on page 6-2 for all documents that may be sent electronically.

Don't use character styles. Many people like to format some of their headings within the paragraph. Unfortunately, this requires not only a paragraph style, but also a character style. You will have to apply the style to the paragraph and then manually select the heading name to format it with a character style.

See Figure 9-1.

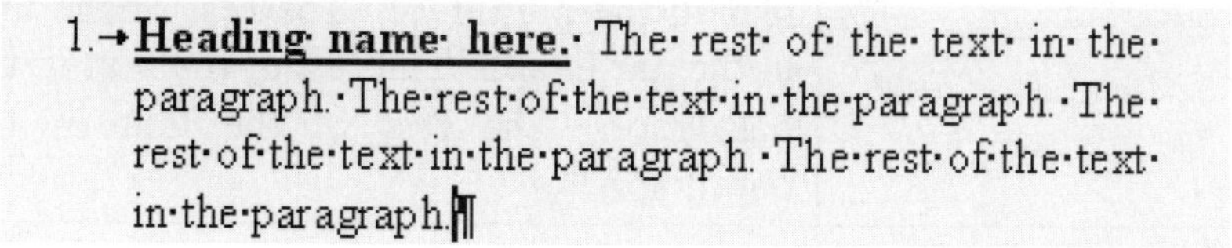

1. **Heading name here.** The rest of the text in the paragraph. The rest of the text in the paragraph. The rest of the text in the paragraph. The rest of the text in the paragraph.

Figure 9-1: Troublesome Heading Format

Styles

Instead, use a layout like the one shown in Figure 9-2. While it may take more paper, it will save you lots of time, particularly if you create lots of documents using this layout.

1. **Heading name here.**¶
   ¶
   The rest of the text in the paragraph. The rest of the text in the paragraph. The rest of the text in the paragraph. The rest of the text in the paragraph.¶

Figure 9-2: Better Alternative Heading Format

Unfortunately, many people are stuck with certain layouts, such as government and legal documents, but if you have anything to say about it, you can save tons of work this way.

Don't use tables to set your headings to the left of the paragraph text, such as shown in Figure 9-3 unless you must.

Heading	Corresponding text here. The rest of the text in the paragraph. The rest of the text in the paragraph. The rest of the text in the paragraph. The rest of the text in the paragraph.
Heading	Corresponding text here. The rest of the text in the paragraph. The rest of the text in the paragraph. The rest of the text in the paragraph. The rest of the text in the paragraph.

Figure 9-3: Troublesome Heading Format

Instead, set your headings to be aligned to the left margin and your paragraph text to be indented, as shown in Figure 9-4.

▪ **Heading**¶
    Corresponding text here. The rest of the text in the paragraph. The rest of the text in the paragraph. The rest of the text in the paragraph. The rest of the text in the paragraph.¶

Figure 9-4: Better Alternative Heading Format

When creating styles for column layouts, where the column may be only a few inches wide, don't justify your text. See Figure 9-5.

While this paragraph may seem to look okay when using short words, try using longer words like "extraordinary" and notice how justifying your text can discombobulate it and make it look very weird. Is "discombobulate" spelled right?¶

Figure 9-5: Troublesome Justification in Columns

Left justifying thin columns just seems to work a bit better, as shown in Figure 9-6.

> While·this·paragraph·may·
> seem·to·look·okay·when·
> using·short·words,·try·using·
> longer·words·like·
> "extraordinary"·and·notice·
> how·justifying·your·text·can·
> discombobulate·it·and·make·
> it·look·very·weird.·Is·
> "discombobulate"·spelled·
> right?¶

Figure 9-6: Better Justification in Columns

For the same reasons, inserting clipart with justified text wrapped around it can look pretty bad. I recently saw a book that had text wrapped around a graphic, and it looked something like Figure 9-7.

Figure 9-7: Troublesome Justification with Pictures

Notice how the word "extraordinary" gets separated. While you can turn on automatic hyphenation, it still breaks the word and does not look nice.

The best way is to just avoid thin columns or avoid placing your graphics along side of the text. Insert it between paragraphs instead.

When the boss tells you that they want the layout a certain way, argue for the methods that will save you time. Money talks, and the boss will want to know that it'll save you lots of time to use your methods. Remember: 10 minutes each workday = one week per year.

Create a Custom Style

Creating a custom style is a great way to keep from changing your normal.dot template. It's also a great way to be sure all the styles you use are easier to pick from—by giving them all names that start with the same letters.

I recently helped a client create custom styles and we named them all so that the first two letters were the same. We also made all the style names begin with a lower-case A so that they would appear alphabetically at the top of the style list.

Sample Text

Creating sample text is easy in any version of Word. For many years, this feature was not documented, but it's still difficult to find. Simply type =rand() and hit enter to create the default of three paragraphs of text, three sentences each.

You can further specify how many paragraphs and how many sentences per paragraph by typing =rand(5,2) for example, to get five paragraphs of two sentences each. Change the number in the parentheses to suit yourself.

Figure 9-8 shows what you get when you type just =rand() into your document:

> The quick brown fox jumps over the lazy dog. The quick brown fox jumps over the lazy dog. The quick brown fox jumps over the lazy dog. The quick brown fox jumps over the lazy dog. The quick brown fox jumps over the lazy dog.¶
>
> The quick brown fox jumps over the lazy dog. The quick brown fox jumps over the lazy dog. The quick brown fox jumps over the lazy dog. The quick brown fox jumps over the lazy dog. The quick brown fox jumps over the lazy dog.¶

Figure 9-8: Sample Text Using =rand()

The text inserted takes the formatting currently in use at the insertion point.

Tip 19: Create a Custom Style

If you use styles or are just learning, you'll love learning how to create new ones of your own.

1. Open a new, blank document by hitting the New Blank Document icon on the Standard toolbar, or Ctrl+N as a keyboard shortcut.

2. Type your name, select the text, and format it in any font you like, any size, with any type of paragraph formatting, underlines, borders, etc.

3. When you are satisfied with it, keep it selected and hit Format→ Style→ New. Type in your name as the name of the style.

4. Hit Ok.

Changing Style Formatting

You've now created a custom style. Suppose you wanted to bold it and forgot to? Simply select it, bold it and then:

- In Word 97 and 2000: Select the style AGAIN from the Style dropdown this time. You'll be asked whether you want to Update the style to reflect recent changes -or- Reapply the formatting of the styles to the selection. You'll choose to Update the style.

- In Word 2002/XP, you'll use the Task Pane to hit the dropdown next to your style and choose Update to match selection.

Styles

> The manual method of changing a style is to hit Format→ Style, choose the style and then hit Modify. There are many settings that you can change within that dialog box.

> To update the Normal style, you MUST use the Style dialog box.

Creating TOCs from Styles

By default, tables of contents are created using heading styles: Heading1, Heading2 and Heading3. Refer to Figure 9-9.

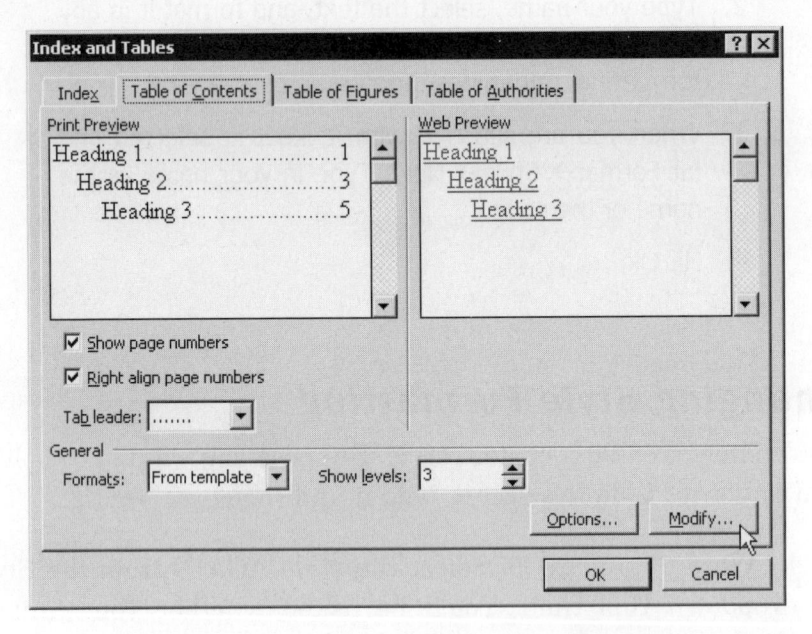

Figure 9-9: Index and Tables Dialog, Table of Contents Tab

If you create custom styles, or wish to use other styles, this is easily accomplished by using the options button under:

> Word 97 and 2000: Insert→Index and Tables→Table of Contents tab.

> Word 2002/XP: Insert→References→Index and Tables→ Table of Contents tab.

Using this method to create a table of contents is by far the easiest method! However, something that commonly occurs is that people create the table of contents and then see the styles TOC1, TOC2, etc., appear in their styles list.

These TOC styles are built-in and created by inserting a table of contents. You should not apply these styles to any text unless, for instance, you're manually adding something to your table of contents.

Even if you're not using a table of contents, creating one can help you to be sure you don't have inappropriate styles set in your document. It wasn't very long ago that my graphics used to show up in my tables of contents because I had the wrong style applied!

Style Organizer

Use the Style Organizer to copy styles (among other things, such as macros and toolbars) from one document or template to another. Simply open the document to which you want to apply the styles.

> Word 97 and 2000: Format→ Style and hit the Organizer button.

> Word 2002/XP: Tools→ Templates and Addins, and hit the Organizer button.

Styles

From here, your document appears on the left panel. On the right panel, the template on which the document was based appears. You can hit the Close File button on the right. The button now reads Open File. Hit it again. Open the file that has the styles you want to store in the current document. Refer to Figure 9-10.

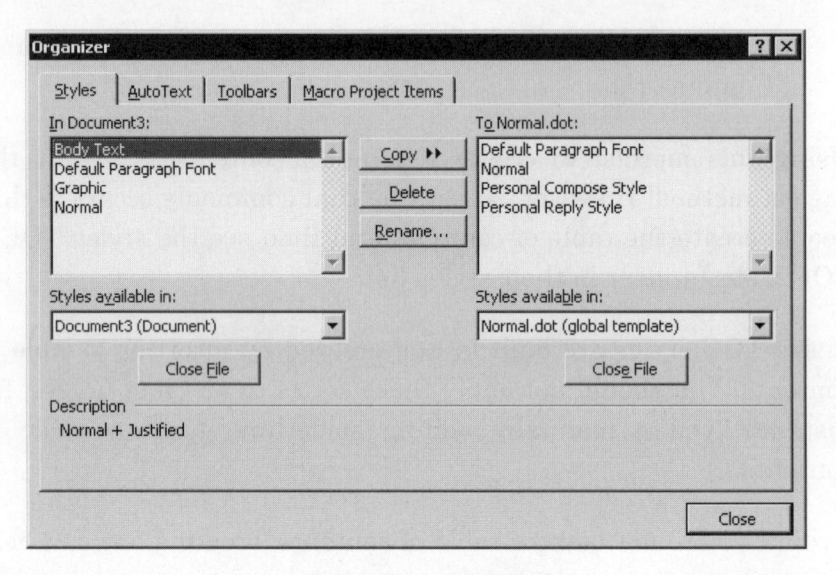

Figure 9-10: Word's Organizer

Select the desired styles from the document on the right-hand side and hit the Copy button to copy them into your document.

9-10   Dreamboat On Word

Styles FAQ

Based on many telephone support calls, here are some of the most common questions and/or issues that arise regarding styles:

Question: I've created a Master/Subdocument structure. Every time I want to pull in a subdocument, I get a message about styles? What does this mean?

Answer: This means that you created multiple subdocuments that were either not based on the same template as the master document (desirable), or the styles were changed in the subdocument, but not in the master or the template.

Whenever you intend to bring documents together into one document, always be sure that you use the exact same styles in all of them prior to inserting them.

If you find yourself in this dilemma, the easiest method to resolve it is to use the Style Organizer. Choose which document has the styles that you really want to use and use the Organizer to copy those styles from the chosen document into the secondary document.

Question: When I paste text from one document to another, it looks different than it did in the source document. Why?

Answer: The text had styles applied in the source document. When you paste it into the new document, the new document's styles are picked up by the text. Try the various Paste Special options (under Edit→Paste Special) to find the result that works best for you.

Styles

Question: Why do I have several different lines or paragraphs formatted as Heading2 style, but they all look different? Or The styles in my document don't match those of the template I'm using.

Answer: Formatting changes have been made to the specific text areas and the style was never updated to include those changes. Whenever creating templates or documents that use specific styles, it's a great idea to go back and check each style. You can do this by clicking on a line with the first style. Choose the style dropdown and pick the style again.

If you get the dialog box asking if you'd like to update it, then changes have been made that were never saved. See Figure 9-11. Ideally, none of your styles will do this while you test. If they do, then just reapply the style.

When sharing templates on a network, make them Read Only so that different users don't inadvertently save changes to the styles in the template.

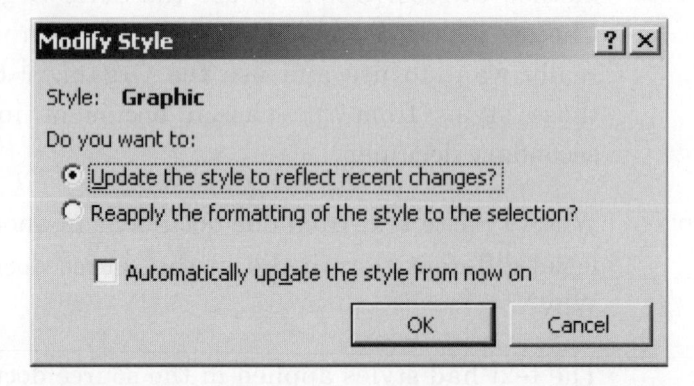

Figure 9-11: Formatting is Changed (Word 97 and Word 2000)

In Word 2002/XP, instead of getting a message, you'll see a changed version of the style added to the style list in the Task Pane. See Figure 9-12.

Styles

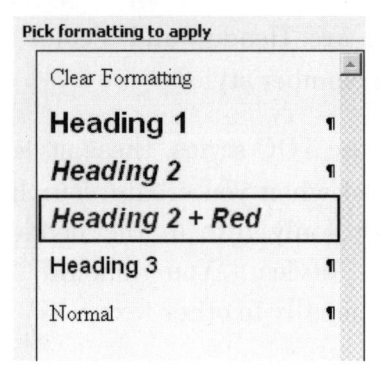

Figure 9-12: Formatting is Changed (Word 2002/XP)

To update the style to include these changes—in this case, to include changing the font color to red—just right-click the original style format and choose the "Update to Match Selection" option, as shown in Figure 9-13.

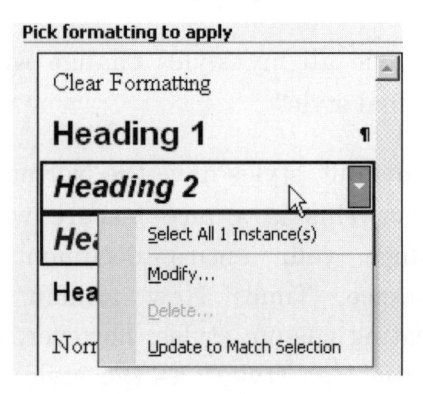

Figure 9-13: Update the Style in Word 2002/XP

Styles

Question: What are Header and Footer styles? What's the Page Number style?

Answer: Like the TOC styles, these styles are automatically created when you create your headers and footers. Ideally, only text in the headers and footers use these styles. You should not apply them intentionally to other text.

Question: When I format some of the text in my document, a whole lot of other parts of my document change formatting as well. What's up with that?

Answer: The style of the paragraph you've selected is set to Automatically update. We personally don't recommend this setting for ANY styles.

Question: Why do all my styles change when I change my Normal style?

Answer: By default, styles have the Normal style underlying them. This is a nice feature when you want to change your entire document text from, for instance, Times New Roman to Arial. When creating custom styles, however, you may want to choose *(no style)* as the style on which to base your new ones.

Figure 9-14 shows the Style dialog box.

9-14   Dreamboat On Word

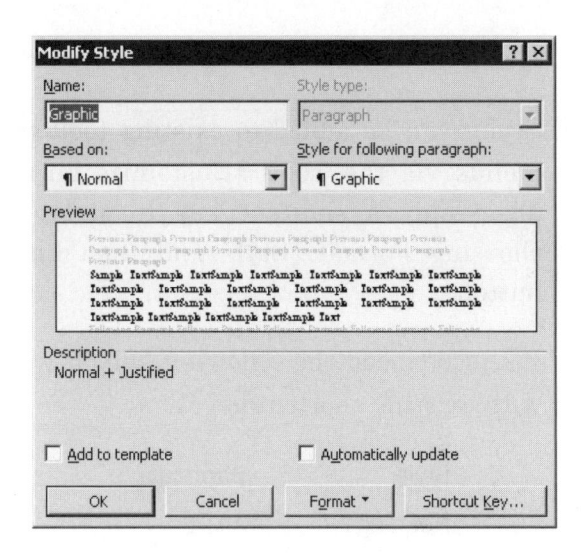

Figure 9-14: Modify Style Dialog Box
(Word 97 and Word 2000)

Question: Why does my spell checker NOT work on certain areas of text?

Answer: Likely, the formatting of the style has language set to "(no proofing)". This is simple to test. Click inside of a paragraph and hit Tools→Language→Set language. Ensure that it is not set for no proofing as shown in Figure 9-15.

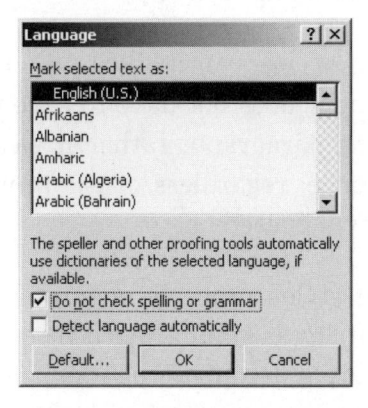

Figure 9-15: No Proofing is Set
(Word 2000 and 2002/XP)

Styles

Question: How can I automate using styles even more?

Answer: Styles can be added to existing toolbars or custom menus via the Tools→Customize button. You can also apply a shortcut key to styles you use by choosing Format→Style and then hit the Modify button.

We recommend the following, which won't interfere with existing shortcut keys:

Style	Shortcut
Heading1	Alt+1
Heading2	Alt+2
Heading3	Alt+3
Bullets	Alt+B
Numbers	Alt+N
Graphics	Alt+G
Captions	Alt+C

Question: Except for Tables of Contents, what benefits are there to using styles?

Answer: Using styles can reduce file size because Word document does not have to save the format settings of each paragraph, rather it saves that formatting only once, regardless of the number of paragraphs the style is used on.

Using styles properly ensures that your document formatting is standardized throughout. Using styles properly in templates can help ensure that everyone uses the proper styles, and/or that all styles in multiple documents use standard formatting.

Larger companies generally have what's called a styles sheet. This document would outline all the fonts, logo graphics, etc., that are appropriately used in the company's printed matter. Style sheets can greatly help to ensure that styles are appropriately applied.

Question: Why would I want to use a style on a graphic?

Answer: Graphics, like any other paragraph, can be formatted to the center of the page, and you can apply space before and after the paragraph (graphic). Format the paragraph style to Keep with next so that your caption below your picture doesn't drop to the next page without the picture.

This page intentionally left blank

10. Bullets and Numbering

Bullets and numbering effectively use the Hanging Indent format described previously. If you are using more than one level of bullets or more than one level of numbering, I strongly suggest you use Styles as described on page 9-1.

Tip 20: Reset Bullets and Numbering

Prior to commencing work on a new file in which you intend to use bullets and numbering, reset each of the bulleted and numbered styles.

1. To reset them, simply hit Format→Bullets and Numbering.
2. Begin with the Bulleted tab. Click once on each bullet style shown and, if it is available, click the Reset button.
3. Do this to each of the bullet styles shown. Of course, Reset is never available for the None style.
4. Do the same thing for the Numbered and Outline Numbered tabs.

Bullets

These days, you can have just about any kind of bullet you want. If your logo looks great when it's very small in size, try using it! Just hit Format→Bullets and Numbering, choose the Bulleted tab and then the button that says Picture.

There are also many, many free fancy bullets available through Clips Online. I am very happy with the way that Microsoft has kept up with that feature. There are so many things to choose from, including bullets, lots of graphics and borders for your newsletters, presentations and other media.

Numbered Lists

Everyone hates Word numbering, including me. It just doesn't seem to work right when we need it to the most. However, if you carefully set up numbering BEFORE you begin formatting, you'll be fine.

Numbered lists aren't difficult to format. Generally, you can just hit the numbering button on the toolbar.

One of the problems you may come across is that the numbering is not in sequential order.

Tip 21: Easiest Way to Fix Numbered or Bulleted Lists

This is so easy you won't believe it. Often, in numbered lists, a number becomes skipped or starts over at 1 again, just use the Format Painter to correct the badly numbered or bulleted paragraphs.

Select the last paragraph that was properly numbered or bulleted. Hit the Format Painter button, which is shown in Figure 10-1.

Figure 10-1: Format Painter Button

> Hitting the Format Painter once turns it on for application to one other area only and it automatically shuts itself off after it's been used.

> Hitting the Format Painter twice turns it on until you click on the button again, or Esc, to turn it off.

Once you've hit the button, the format is "copied." Click once anywhere in another paragraph and the same formatting is applied to it.

Be careful not to select portions of the paragraphs because it will format only selections. It works best to simply click once anywhere inside the paragraph.

Dreamboat On Word

Bullets and Numbering

Outline Numbering

Outline numbering can be very difficult. The good news is that you can overcome the difficulties! I have had several people tell me that my methods don't work. For each one of those people, I've had dozens that tell me the methods work great. You decide.

For documents that have previously been formatted and the formatting just won't work, please see Formatting Outline Numbered Templates below.

Formatting Outline Numbered Headings

Some documents—military documents are a good example—have every paragraph numbered. This makes it easy for them to refer to later. You can also bookmark them and cross-reference them. Then, if an item's number changes because you inserted another item, the cross-reference stays linked with the correct paragraph.

To format outline numbering for headings:

1. Go to Format→ Bullets and Numbering

2. Choose an outline numbering that shows headings.

    (Remember that you should reset all of your numbering styles in this dialog before you begin!)

3. Hit the Customize button.

4. Click on each numbering level in the left-hand column and set the indents and space between numbers and text as desired.

5. Hit Ok.

> Notes: *Some numbering schemes have lengthy numbers that take up a lot of space. For instance, an item numbered 10.12.22.4 that is followed by a half-*

10-4   Dreamboat On Word

> *inch indent can take up quite a bit of the body width of your document.*
>
> *Your paragraph of text is now indented considerably and an otherwise short paragraph can take up a lot more page length.*
>
> *Using Outline numbering for your heading styles is not recommended unless it meets the requirements of your company or firm, or if your document is limited to perhaps Heading 3 or 4.*

To use the first level of that outline numbering, your text must begin on the left margin. To use level 2, hit Tab or use the Increase Indent button on the toolbar, and then type your text. To use level 3, hit Tab again, and so on. Use Shift+Tab to decrease your indent to the previous level.

Not only does using Tab and Shift+Tab increase and decrease your paragraph indent, it also changes the style formatting on the paragraph. Watch it switch from Heading 1 to Heading 2 and so on as you Tab or Shift+Tab.

Formatting Outline Numbered Templates

Now suppose you've struggled over three or four Heading outline numbered documents, and now you want to continue with these better methods.

1. In a new document, type some sample text for heading levels 1, 2, 3, and 4, or however many levels you used in your document.

2. Format them as outline numbered using the method above.

3. If this is exactly how you wanted it to look the first time around, save this file as a template. Close it.

4. Open one of your badly formatted documents.

Bullets and Numbering

5. Hit Format→ Style and hit the Organizer button. Your document's styles appear in the left-hand side of the window. On the right, you'll see normal.dot.

6. Close normal.dot with the Close button. The Close button turns into an Open button. Hit it and open your new outline numbered template.

7. Copy whatever styles you created in your template over to your existing document.

8. Close the template.

9. Hit OK. All of your previous heading styles should now be replaced with appropriately outline numbered heading styles.

11. Borders and Shading

People often call or write about having to get rid of a line in their document that "just appeared"...wasn't inserted intentionally. This is a border and it's generally created because of the settings under Autoformat As You Type, described in Options Settings beginning on page 3-16.

Tip 22: Get Rid of Unwanted Borders

To get rid of an unwanted border, simply select several paragraphs above the border down to several paragraphs below the border, and hit Format→Borders and Shading, choose the Borders tab and then None.

That generally works. I have actually requested that people simply select all (Ctrl+A) and remove the borders that way, and then add the borders back where they really want them.

Often, if you try selecting only one paragraph, you'll try to remove the top border, only to end up with the border having now moved to the bottom.

Page Borders

Page borders are pretty self-explanatory. However, I constantly see a couple of the same questions about this over and over, which really don't have to do with the feature, and you'll see why.

A lot of people want to add to the page borders that are available. I know of no way to add to the page border formats available in the Page Border dialog box.

If you want a custom border, create your own in any graphics program, or Insert→ Picture→Clipart and choose from the many page borders available online. If you create your own, you'll want to make the border graphic the same size as the paper you're printing on.

Go to View→Header and Footer. Hit Insert→Picture, choose Clipart or From File, and choose your graphic border. After inserting it, double-click it to ensure that it is the same size as your paper and position it to exactly align with the top-left corner of your page. Also be sure that you've formatted it to be BEHIND text.

This method puts a page border on every page. If you only want a page border on a certain page, you'll have to handle it as you would any other page that would contain a different header. See Tables on page 12-1.

Other Borders

Figure 11-1 shows the Borders dialog box. From here, you can place borders on selected paragraphs, on selected words, or on the cells of a table.

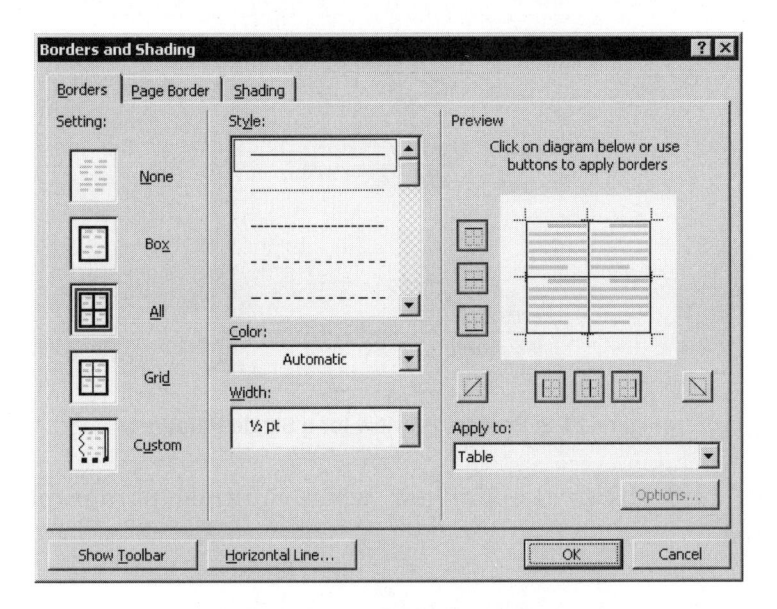

Figure 11-1: Borders Dialog Box for a Table

Prior to taking the above screen shot, I selected a table that already had borders applied on all cells so that you could see the preview of the borderlines that run vertically and horizontally through the middle.

Note how the borders in use in the preview are displayed around the preview. Clicking these buttons removes or applies the individual borderlines to the area shown in the Apply To box at the bottom.

Depending on the selection you make before choosing Format→ Borders and Shading, a different preview is shown.

Figure 11-2 shows the preview when a single paragraph is selected.

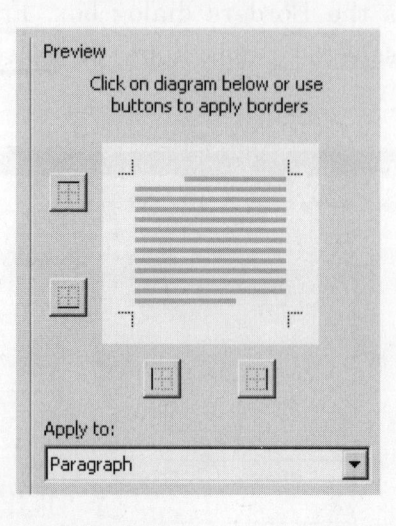

Figure 11-2: Borders Preview for a Single Paragraph

Figure 11-3 shows the preview when multiple paragraphs are selected.

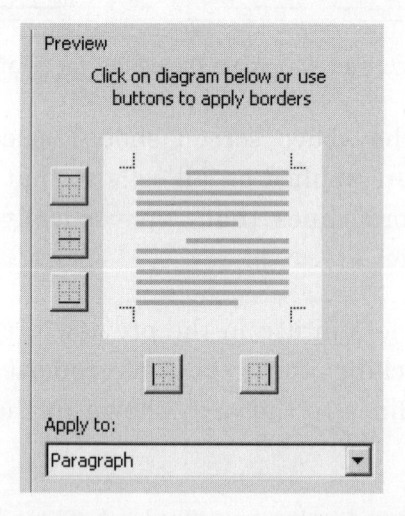

Figure 11-3: Border Preview for Multiple Paragraphs

Finally, Figure 11-4 shows the preview when only words are selected.

Borders and Shading

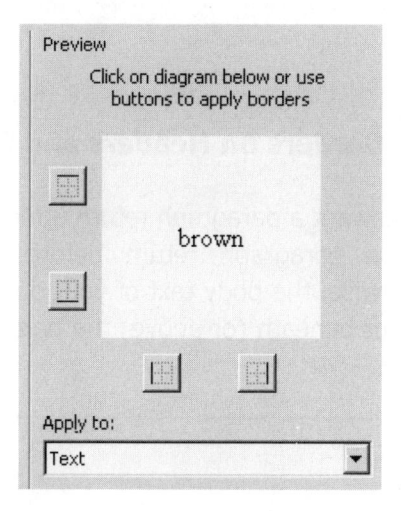

Figure 11-4: Border Preview for Words

Unfortunately, and even though the dialog leads users to believe that they can, you cannot use only one of the borderlines around words within a paragraph. If you choose any of the four border buttons shown in the Preview, you'll get the same results:

brown

Borders can be used to format styles so that, for instance, all of your Heading 1 style text can be centered inside of a box on a page, like this:

My Chapter Title

See how to create Styles on page 9-1. Borders are a nice way to break up the important areas of your document.

Borders in Headers and Footers

Use borders in your headers and footers to separate the body text from the header and footer.

Borders and Shading

Tip 23: Borders on Headers and Footers

Note that you want a paragraph return after your Header border and a paragraph return before your Footer border. Otherwise, the body text of your document could be placed right beneath (or above) the border, as shown in Figure 11-5.

Figure 11-5: Improper Borders in Headers and Footers

You'll want it to look like Figure 11-6 instead.

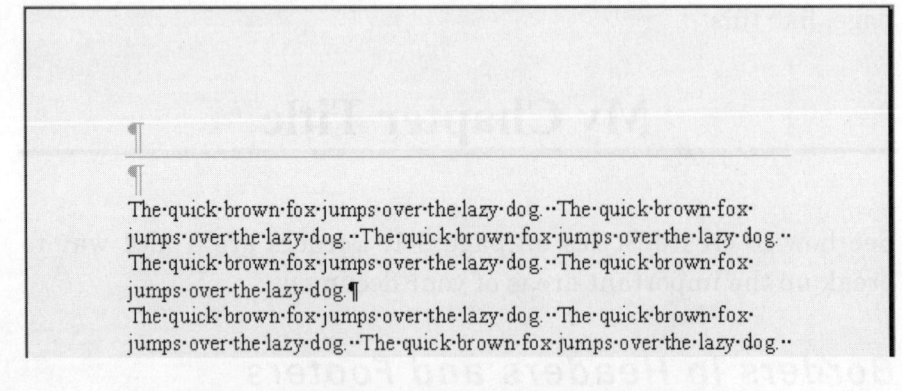

Figure 11-6: Proper Borders in Headers and Footers

12. Tables

Tables in Microsoft Word can be one of the hardest features to understand and troubleshoot. People use them and don't know how and, much to our dismay, people don't use them when they should.

Tables should be used to create lists and to lay out text or other document components side-by-side. A review of many brochures, magazines and books demonstrates that tables are used quite often. Many web pages are laid out with the use of tables.

Creating Tables in Word

All options regarding tables are found under the Table menu. There is also a Tables and Borders toolbar that can be used by choosing View→Toolbars→Tables and Borders.

Tables can be inserted or drawn into a document. The rectangles that make up a table are called cells. With the Show/Hide toolbar button on, a symbol is displayed at the end of the text in each cell; these are called end-of-cell markers.

Figure 12-1: Show/Hide Toolbar Button

Figure 12-2: End-of-Cell Marker

Tables

Tables are broken down into rows (horizontal) and columns (vertical). Individual rows and columns can easily be selected using the mouse pointer and click-and-drag, or they can be selected through the Table menu options.

Some of the many properties of a table that can be changed are:

➢ Cell margins. This is the distance between the contents of the cell and the border or edge of the cell	➢ Text direction. Text can be turned sideways to the left or sideways to the right using Format☐Text Direction.
➢ Splitting and Merging cells.	➢ Row height and Column width.
➢ Splitting cells diagonally.	➢ Filling cells with colors and patterns.

The preceding is formatted as a two-column, three-row table.

A tour through the Table→Properties options helps you to find the many settings that can be changed. Be sure your cursor is inside of a table or that specific items are selected if menu items are unavailable (grayed out).

A review of Format→Borders and Shading is useful. In addition, a review of the Table sorting commands makes you a better troubleshooter. You need to understand how the sorting commands work, whether with a table or just a list of text in a document.

Tip 24: Sorting Text Without a Table

Because the Sort option is only available under the Table menu, many people believe you cannot sort text that does NOT reside in a table. This is not true! While your text must be formatted properly, it doesn't have to be in a table. For best results, you only need to be sure that you have one tab between each column in your sort.

Refer to Figure 12-3 to follow the steps.

FirstName   LastName
Mickey   Mouse
Donald   Duck
Road   Runner
Wiley   Coyote

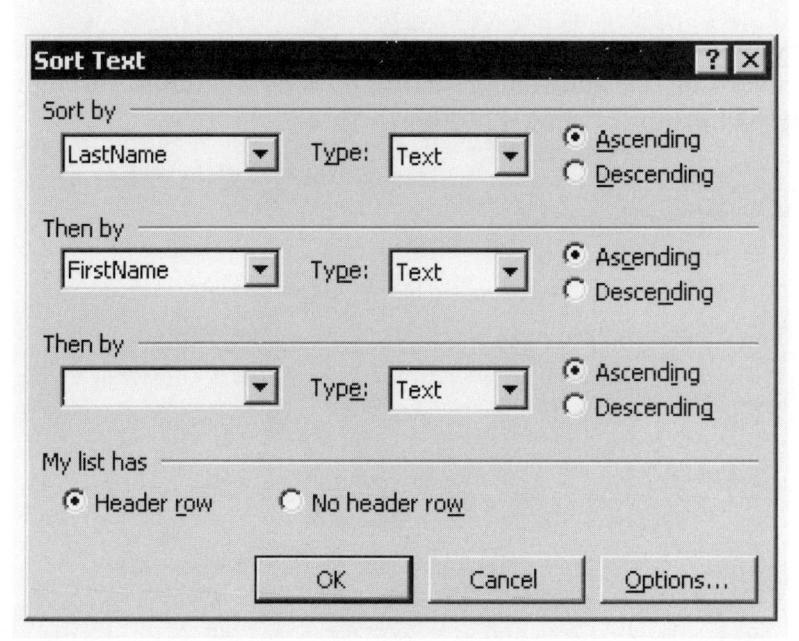

Figure 12-3: Sort Text Dialog Box

Tables

Create a list of first and last names:

1. Type the word "FirstName," hit Tab.
2. Type the word "LastName," hit Enter.
3. Type a first name and hit Tab. Type a last name and hit enter.
4. Repeat until you have five or six names. Be sure the names are not already in alphabetical order by last name so you can see how this feature works. You may want to change the tab settings to align the columns correctly.

> Note: *Do NOT use extra tabs to properly align the columns or the sort feature does not work.*

5. With your cursor placed just to the left of the FirstName heading, hit Table→Sort.
6. At the bottom of the dialog, choose Header row. Then choose your Sort by options above it.

Be aware of the additional sorting options available through the Options button, as shown in Figure 12-4.

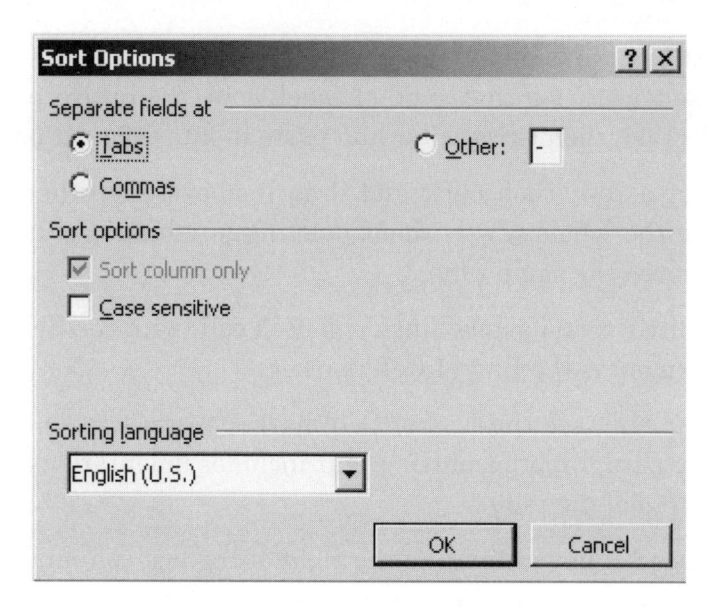

Figure 12-4: Sort Options Dialog Box

Many people are either unaware of the Sort feature in Word or believe that it works only for sorting data in tables.

Quick Facts About Tables

- Tables can often be used instead of column formatting. This is particularly true for layout of brochures, booklets and newsletters. Any layout that requires columns can often be accomplished using tables, which are much less of a headache than columns can be.
- Hitting Tab within a cell makes the cursor jump to the next cell.
- Hitting Ctrl+Tab creates the tab within the cell.
- To create a new row at the bottom of a table, put the cursor in the last existing cell and hit Tab.
- To create a new page of labels, put the cursor in the last label and hit Tab until the entire next page is filled with labels.

- Most label layouts are done with tables. If holding the tab key doesn't work for that type of label, copy the entire page, hit Ctrl+End, then Ctrl+Enter and paste it onto the next page.
- Select a row, then click and drag it above any other row to move the whole row without deleting anything. Columns can be moved the same way.
- The little round symbol inside of each cell (with the Show/Hide button on) is the End-of-Cell marker.
- If you can't see the End-of-Cell marker in your table, there is likely paragraph formatting that includes indentations outside the area of the table.
- To insert a new column to the right of the last column in Word 97, select the End-of-Cell markers to the far right of the table as you would select a column. Hit Table→Insert→Row.
- In Word 97, you must remove the Float Over Text option to position a graphic inside of a table cell.
- Gridlines are viewed and borders are printed. In Word 6.0, tables do NOT have borders by default. In Word 97, 2000 and 2002/XP they have borders by default.
- To test for proper formatting of a table, copy it and paste it into Excel. If Excel maintains the layout, the table is perfectly formatted. Merged cells and missing data reduces the likelihood of proper layout.
- By default in Word 6.0, 97 and 2000, a new document containing a table is used as the Data Source when using the Mail Merge Helper. Excel usually is the better option, however, because of its easier sorting capabilities and because a many-column data source may extend the document size in Word. Word 2002/XP uses Access as its default data source. See more on Mail Merge on page 17-1.

When to Use

Some of the following uses of tables in Word might be considered workarounds, but they're excellent and you may find that you already use these layouts. You do not have to use the borders; we have used them to demonstrate the layout.

Displaying Data

Use tables to display data, as shown in Figure 12-5. This use is common in all types of documents.

Product	Price for 1	Price for 2	Price for 3
Jelly Beans	.01	.02	.03
Candy Bars	.60	1.20	1.80

Figure 12-5: Data Display

Headings Left/Text Right

Use tables to layout headings on the left with text on the right, as shown in Figure 12-6. Some people particularly like this layout for manuals and for resumes. This layout is also commonly used to display graphics or photos on the left and text on the right.

First Heading Text	The quick brown fox jumps over the lazy dog. The quick brown fox jumps over the lazy dog. The quick brown fox jumps over the lazy dog. The quick brown fox jumps over the lazy dog. The quick brown fox jumps over the lazy dog.
Second Heading Text	The quick brown fox jumps over the lazy dog. The quick brown fox jumps over the lazy dog. The quick brown fox jumps over the lazy dog. The quick brown fox jumps over the lazy dog.

Figure 12-6: Headings on Left, Text on Right

Lists

Use tables to layout long, bulleted lists, as shown in Figure 12-7.

• Software	• Hardware	• Printers	• Training
• Support	• Knowledge	• Manuals	• Internet

Figure 12-7: Bulleted Lists

Headers and Footers

Use tables in headers and footers as displayed in

Figure 12-8. This is especially helpful when considering the layout below. The table forces the height of the line to be higher than the text. Without the table, the "Part 1" text would appear too low because it would align with the bottom of the manual title instead of the top of the manual title.

Microsoft Word	**Part 1**
Troubleshooting Manual	**Tables**

Figure 12-8: Using Tables in Headers and Footers

Creative Uses for Tables

Tables can be very helpful for formatting a variety of commonplace objects. Be creative.

- You want to place four graphic objects evenly on a page.
    1. Insert a two-row, two-column table.
    2. Size the rows so that they take up the whole page. You can get an exact measurement without using points. Just type, for instance, 5" and Word converts it to points for you.
    3. Use paragraph alignment to have the graphics placed properly.
    4. The graphics need to be formatted as In Line With Text.

- You want to have signature lines at the bottom of every document, as for a contract or agreement.
    1. Insert a two-row, three-column table.
    2. Make the center column about a half-inch.
    3. Be sure the first and third columns are of equal width to each other.
    4. In the bottom row, type in the words "Signature" and "Date", etc.
    5. Put a border only on the line between the rows and only on the first and third columns.
    6. To further automate the task, select this table and create an AutoText entry (see page 4-3).

- You want to create a form that is to be filled out by handwriting, such as a sign-in sheet.
    1. Create a one-row, one-column table.
    2. Select the row and make it 16 points high.
    3. Put a border on the bottom of the cell only.
    4. Hit Tab until the rows fill the page.

> You want to create a list in two- or three-columns.

 1. Create a two- or three-column table.
    Many people select a list and put it into a two- or three-column (not table) layout. This produces section breaks in a document, which can be confusing. Placing lists in a table produces much better results.

When Not to Use Tables

There are several mistakes commonly made when creating tables. I've listed them here, along with the appropriate way to get the desired results. Some problems occur more with Word 97 than with higher versions.

Tables as Document or Manual Layouts

People use tables to set up entire documents, particularly for the Header Left/Text Right layout. They run into problems later, however, because they want to add text and this pushes the tables onto the next page, producing undesirable results.

More than likely, the user is creating huge paragraphs of text within rows of tables, which creates rows that are several inches high or may even span more than one page. Unless the manual or document is made up of simple, short paragraphs, and each paragraph is in its own row, the Header Left/Text Right layout is not desirable.

Convert the table to text by using Table→Convert Table to Text. Place the headings above the text, using the manner in which this document is laid out, or place the headings in a textbox and use indented text for the body text.

Tables That Have Merged Cells

Many people layout a table and then merge cells in the headings. After doing that, they decide to insert a new column and it just doesn't work. Sometimes, it can affect the entire table. The only way to describe what happens is to say that the columns become offset.

Select a column by placing the cursor above the middle of the first row of the column. The cursor turns into a small, black, down-pointing arrow (similar to ↓). When clicked, the column becomes selected.

If cells from two or more columns become selected, then this table's columns have become offset. If this happens, try to delete the rows that comprise the headings and recreate them. Otherwise, try converting the table to text by using Table→Convert Table to Text, and then, while keeping the text selected, convert it back to a table again by using Table→ Convert Text to Table.

Converting Tables to Text or Text to Tables

This is often not as easy as we would like it to be. We always want the impossible. We want to take a mail-merged label file and convert it into a mail merge data source for another purpose. That's when we ask: What has happened to the original data source? And find we deleted it or never had it in the first place, as would be the case if. someone e-mailed you the label format. Unfortunately, converting this to text and back to a table is rarely easy.

Assuming the labels are laid out in a similar fashion to the one shown in Figure 12-9, there are some definite steps that need to be taken.

Tables

Name Title Company Address3 Address4	Name Address1 Address2 Address3 Address4	Name Address1 Address3 Address4
Name Address1 Address2 Address3 Address4	Name Address1 Address2 Address4	Name Name Address2 Address3 Address4

Figure 12-9: Address Label Layout

Here, I was going to provide you with a long, drawn-out dissertation on how to get this data into a database format. However, we have some Visual Basic for Applications code that performs this task for you! The code and how to use it are provided in the sample macro on page 21-12.

13. Section Breaks

There's just no way to describe the frustration and aggravation that many users of Word have when trying to set up proper headers and footers. To get around the anomalies, I've seen people use textboxes, put section breaks on every page, and all sorts of other workarounds. Here, I share the secrets that make this process easy. I describe the different section breaks, when to use them, and how to get control of your headers and footers.

What are Breaks for?

Under the Insert→Break menu, there are several types of breaks. They control your page layout and affect the use of headers and footers from one page/section to the next. To test some of the information provided below, you'll want to have your Show/Hide button on.

Types of Breaks and When to Use

Page Break

Page breaks are easily inserted by hitting Ctrl+Enter on your keyboard. Instead of hitting the Enter key a number of times to get your cursor to the top of the next page, use Ctrl+Enter instead. This inserts a manual page break.

The problems with using paragraph returns to get to the next page are these:

➢ If you later add text somewhere, you must readjust all of the paragraph returns so that your text isn't all moved down.

Section Breaks

> Some printers print differently than others. If you use a page break, the text on the next page is sure to print at the top of the page.
>
> If you use paragraph returns, the printer driver may actually shift these up or down. The longer the document, the worse the shifting will be.

It is not necessary to use page breaks in your documents at all. Certain paragraph formatting provides for some of the reasons we use page breaks.

For instance, if I want to ensure that the text in my paragraph above stays with the bullets that follow it, regardless of how much text I insert on pages above it, I would click inside that paragraph, hit Format→Paragraph, choose the Line and Page Breaks tab and choose the Keep with Next option. This keeps the paragraph return on the same page as the next paragraph return.

When discussing styles, I said that you would not need to use paragraph returns to put space between your paragraphs. This is the perfect example to explain why an additional paragraph return between the above paragraph and its following bullets does not work well with other Word features.

Here, the Keep with Next only ensures that the leading paragraph of text would stay on the same page with the paragraph return that is used for spacing between paragraphs and not with the next bulleted item's paragraph return.

Column Break

This break simply allows you to move to the top of the next column in a newsletter or other column layout. When you have not set any columns, Word still provides a one-column layout. So, in effect, a column break works as a page break when you have not formatted to use multiple columns.

Text Wrapping Break

The text below a text-wrapping break is forced to drop below the item being wrapped around. This is great to use when you're starting a new paragraph while the text is wrapping, and it would not look right to have the first sentence cut off.

Next-Page Section Break

The least confusing section break is the next-page section break. It combines a section break with a page break. It allows you to change headers and footers from one page or group of pages to the next.

By default, the next-page section break assigns the headers and footers to be Same as Previous. I provide more information about this later in this section.

Continuous Section Break

If I had my way, this section break type would not exist. Suppose you have a long list of bullets and you would like them to appear side by side instead of vertically down the page. Above the list, you can insert a continuous section break, format the bulleted list area to be a two- or three-column layout, insert another continuous section break below the bulleted list, and then format back to a one-column layout.

Section Breaks

Likewise, if you were to select the bulleted list and then format a multi-column layout, Word would automatically insert the continuous section breaks for you.

So why don't we like them? Virtually any column layout you might want to use is much more easily produced in a Word table, while avoiding confusion about the number of sections in your document. If you have a 300-page document with 7 chapters, you'll have 8 sections, the first section being the cover page and Table of Contents.

If you have 3 areas of column formats, you'll have 11 sections. This would drive even the best Word desktop publishers insane trying to figure out which section and chapter they're working in.

Even-Page Section Break

Suppose you are using a duplex printed layout. Duplex means you're printing the document two-sided. You may want every new Chapter of your manual to start on an even page or left-hand page. This is highly unlikely; so we'll save the description of this, which is similar, for the next section break type.

Odd-Page Section Break

More likely to be used than an even-page, the odd-page section break is like a next-page section break, except that it forces the page number to be that of the next available odd page number. Suppose our chapter 2 is 9 pages long. It began on page 11 and ended on page 19. We want the next chapter to start on the next odd page, or page 21. Inserting an odd-page section break makes that occur.

Tip 25: Avoid Odd-Page Section Breaks

Okay, so I'm not crazy about this section break either. Why? I'll tell you:

- Some printers do not recognize the appropriate duplex printing commands of Word. Hence, you are forced to insert any blank pages that may exist. In our example above, page 20 would not even exist. So your duplex print job could get all messed up by printing page 21 on the back of page 19 instead of making a blank page 20.

- If you're printing this document and copying it with a duplex copier, again, you won't have the blank page 20 to insert and print onto the back of page 19. So you could easily waste tons of paper.

What's our workaround? Use regular next-page section breaks instead. It is far nicer to have the blank page and, perhaps, a statement like "This page intentionally left blank," than to deal with the issues above. As you move from one page to the next, you'll know exactly where you are.

If you're an experienced Word user, perhaps you understand these issues. But what happens when you move onto another job or get a promotion? The person who takes your place must also know of these anomalies.

This page intentionally left blank.

14. Page Numbering

Page numbering often seems more difficult than it really is. It is not the page numbering that makes it difficult, but the creation of proper section breaks that causes the problem.

Inserting Page Numbers

Tip 26: Easiest Page Numbering Method

It appears that most people use the Insert→Page Numbers menu to insert page numbers. This, in fact, puts the page number into a text box. The text box is easily dragged around on the page and sometimes actually gets lost. It also makes it difficult to delete the page numbers.

Instead simply use the # sign symbol button on the Header/Footer toolbar to insert your page numbers.

The button is shown in Figure 14-1.

Figure 14-1: Page Number as Text

Read about section breaks on page 13-1 prior to inserting your page numbers.

The method described in Tip 26 places the page number into your header or footer as though you had typed it in normally at the insertion point. When you use Insert→Page Numbers, choose Right alignment. When you then select the page number, it looks like Figure 14-2.

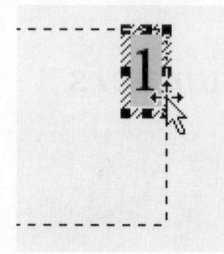

Figure 14-2: Page Number in a Text Box

To delete page numbers when they're formatted like the one in the figure, you must be sure to select the textbox and not just the page number. I've seen many documents with several of these textboxes left lying around inside headers and footers. They can keep your other header and footer content from displaying and printing properly.

Formatting Page Numbers

In this case, the word "format" does not refer to the appearance of the page numbers, but the placement of them.

Figure 14-3: Format Page Number Toolbar Button

Using our preferred method of page numbering, you'll align the page number wherever you like by using the alignment buttons on the Formatting toolbar.

In other words, align just as you would any other text. The Format Page Number button is more useful for telling the page numbering where it should begin numbering.

Tip 27: How to Set Up Typical Page Numbering Sets

To have page numbering begin on the 2nd page and continue numbering throughout the document:

- File→Page setup and choose Different First Page from the Layout tab. Do this BEFORE you insert your headers and footers.
- Insert the page number.

To have page numbering start on the first page of each chapter or section:

- Set up section breaks in your document. You need a section break on the last page of each section.
- Insert the page number and choose to "Start at" Page 1. Depending on your header/footer settings, you may need to do this in each section.

To include Chapter numbers in your page numbering:

- You must first use a heading style, preferably Heading 1. You must also have the heading style numbered, preferably using Outline numbering.
- You must not use the style for any other purpose except as Chapter titles.
- Hit the Insert Page Numbers button on the header/footer toolbar and choose to "Include Chapter Number."

This page intentionally left blank.

15. Templates and Desktop Publishing

I actually "ran into" Word and immediately had to dive into this area of it. I'd been hired to create many manuals. For 2-½ years, all I did was format templates and documents. When I started that job, I had no clue how to use Word. I'd been a WordPerfect user. (Yes. I admit it.)

If you are reading this section, then I strongly encourage you to also read the section on Styles on page 9-1. Styles are an integral part of creating a great template.

Word Templates

Templates are often misunderstood. People create a "boilerplate" document and they use it over and over. They call it a template. Word does not. Word only considers a template a "real" template if the document has been saved as a document template (*.DOT) file. Using a document like a template and changing the file extension does NOT make Word treat your template properly.

There was once a virus that caused Word templates to behave improperly. After that, many people who did not use Word's template feature properly blamed the problems on the virus when, in fact, they were opening the templates and saving them, and complaining that they could not then save them as documents.

A true template has been saved as a document template. It is accessed by using File→New and double-clicking it, or it is double-clicked via Windows Explorer. When either of these occurs, a proper template creates a copy of itself and has a default name like any other document of Document1, Document2 or whichever new document you're creating in this session of Word.

Tip 28: Make Desktop Shortcuts to your Templates

Perhaps you use various templates regularly and don't like having to hit File→New to access them.

Go to Tools→Options, File locations tab. Note the location of your User Templates. Using Windows Explorer, browse to that folder. Right-click the template you use most and choose Copy. Right-click your Desktop, and choose Paste Shortcut. You can then right-click the shortcut and choose Rename to give it any name you want.

If you open a document template and try to save it as a document, you'll be disappointed—it's not possible.

Tip 29: Change a Template to a Document

So, what do you do when you've already accidentally created a new document in your actual template file? Of course, you don't want to lose it, but you don't want to overwrite your template either.

Save the template—as a template—to a new name. Do not attempt to save it elsewhere. Close the template. Hit File→New and choose your new template. Save the file as a document. Delete the newly created template.

Workgroup Templates

Do not forget that if you expect others to be able to view the document in the same manner as you do, they must have access to the template. Choose Tools→Options→File Locations; then choose Workgroup templates to find the location in which you want to store them.

If you don't have one, ask your network administrators to give you a shared location for this purpose, enter that location in the Workgroup templates box (on everybody's PC) and then store the templates in that folder. They'll show up when you hit File→New.

Layout Forethoughts

If you have anything to say about the process of creating the manual before it is written, do so!

Here are just a few things that you can do to make your task much easier:

➢ If you are not the writer, or not the only writer, teach the writers how to create keyboard shortcuts for using styles. As much as you do, they also want to have a good idea of the layout of the information they're providing. Not only that, but a writer may want to use the Outline view to outline the content.

➢ While it's being written, you can be designing a layout. Think about your audience. The younger or less educated supposedly require less text per page and more graphics, while more-educated persons such as engineers are less likely to be distracted when reading large amounts of text without the need for pictures.

Booklets and Newsletter Layouts

Word has never had a nice way to create a booklet layout. This layout, for instance, would be for a letter-size document turned landscape and then folded in half.

Those who might be looking for a nice way to do it—don't bother. I know of only one template and it is set up for a 4-sheet, 16-page layout.

Not only would you drive yourself crazy trying to figure out which page you're on, but also the text boxes are set to continue from one to the next. While it prints correctly, it's a nightmare for the creator.

I strongly suggest that you create any layout on a normal paper size, print it on a great printer, cut it up, tape it together with that Post-it Note type of tape (not permanently sticky) and reproduce it on a printer that's capable of reducing it to the desired size.

The only thing you need to remember about a booklet layout is that it should total a number of pages that is divisible by four. One sheet of paper makes four pages, two sheets makes 8 pages, and so on. Printers call this one sheet a "signature."

After you've created a 16-page layout, print the pages. Then you can put your pages together as shown in the table below. If you pick up on the algorithm used, you'll be able to figure out the layout for any number of pages, as long as they're divisible by four.

Signature #	Side 1 (outside)		Side 2 (inside)	
	Left	Right	Left	Right
1	16	1	2	15
2	14	3	4	13
3	12	5	6	11
4	10	7	8	9

As you can see, an important piece of the layout is that you start with the cover pages on side 1 of signature 1 and then your last signature ends with the centerfold on side 2.

Two-Sided Page Setup

- Determine the page layout. If it's over 100 pages, I strongly recommend printing it two-sided. You'll save money by using less paper and your document won't look intentionally bloated. You may not want to do a two-sided print job if you want to allow the backside of the paper for notes.

- Choose "Different Odd and Even pages" in the Layout tab of File→Page Setup.
This way, you can have your opposing pages set up properly. Think about the person who quickly wants to skim through to find a certain area of the printed document without having to open the pages up to find the reference they're looking for in the header or footer.

- If your page numbers are not centered, you'll always want your odd-number pages/right-hand pages to have the page numbers on the right side of the page, and your even-numbered pages/left-hand pages to have the page numbers on the left side of the page.

➢ If it's being put into a binder, be sure you add a gutter margin (at least one-quarter inch) to the page layout and use the Mirror feature.

➢ You'll always want to account for front and back of each sheet. I don't recommend using Word's feature for having your page numbering start on an even or odd page because not all printers are capable of printing it this way.

Even if they are, if you happen to take your file to a print house to be printed, they may not be aware of the feature and you'll end up with printing on pages that should have been blank.

➢ For best results, whenever a sheet is intentionally left blank, create a page for it that says that. Then, the recipient of the printed document won't fear that there was a printing error in his copy. The generally accepted statement is simple: "This page intentionally left blank."

Tip 30: Same Section—Multiple Documents

So you have hundreds of manuals to maintain, one for each specific bicycle that your company sells. Many parts of the manuals are updated from time to time, such as warranty information. How the heck do you change 100 files at one time?

You can use the Find/Replace, but it's kind of tough getting paragraphs of text into those boxes in the Find/Replace dialog.

A little forethought goes a long way here.

- Create a document that contains the warranty information only.
- Copy the text.
- Open the first manual. In the area of the document where you want the warranty information to appear, hit Edit→Paste Special→Paste link.
- Follow the same steps in each of your manuals.

Next time you update the warranty document, you'll see that all of your documents are now updated.

Stationery Template Layouts

I've found many people creating stationery layouts and struggling with them. I've decided to share this information with you because it's not that difficult to do.

I'm assuming you know how to set up page margins and other simpler tasks.

Letterhead

Just about anyone can create a letterhead template. But can you make the second page work properly for you? Most people have pre-printed stationery with their letterhead/logo printed on it and then blank paper for second and subsequent pages. It's so easy to set this up—you won't believe it.

Tip 31: Create a Letterhead Template

Start with a blank document.

1. Measure the print area of your stationery, both the letterhead and the blank sheets.

2. Set your page margins to work for your BLANK stationery—not your letterhead.

3. Hit Ctrl+Enter to insert a page break.

4. Hit File→Page Setup, Layout tab. Choose Different First Page.

5. Hit Ctrl+Home to go to the top of your document, then View→Header and Footer.

6. Hit Enter until the "At" line in the status bar places your cursor about ¼-inch above the location where you want your text to begin on your letterhead.

7. Hit the Show Next button on the Header/Footer toolbar. Hit Enter again as many times as necessary until the status bar reads ¼-inch above the measurement where you want your text to begin on the second page.

8. Close the Header/Footer toolbar.

9. Delete the page break you created. Save your file as a template in the default location.

10. Set the document to print the first and subsequent pages to the appropriate printer trays (File→Page Setup→Paper Source).

11. Save the template again and close it.

12. To use it, hit File→New.

Yes, there is hope for lawyers, accountants and others who have partner names or other information running down the side of their letterhead. Set the letterhead page as described above. Add the following steps in front of Step 6, above.

6a. To keep the first page from printing on top of the left-hand column (or right-hand—adjust as necessary), yet still allow the second page to print without that large margin, we have to fake-out Word.

6b. While in the header, draw a rectangle sized as tall as your paper, and place it in the approximate position of the pre-printed column area. Format the drawn object to wrap text. Remove any border from the rectangle and, of course, make it white or use No Fill.

Envelopes

The main problem people have with envelopes is setting them to print to the proper printer tray. I've described how to create envelope templates in Features I Could Live Without on page 5-1, so I won't repeat myself.

Business Cards

If you're using Avery or some other pre-packaged business cards, you'll be like most people and have a problem placing your graphics on them. So don't.

Tip 32: Create a Business Card Template

These instructions work for labels, nametags or anything in a label format with a graphic on it.

1. Start with a business card layout by choosing Tools→Envelopes and Labels.

2. Choose the Labels tab, then Options and pick your product from the list.

3. When you're done with that, hit the New Document button. This should give you a 10-card business card layout.

4. For best results, work only in the first business card. If necessary, split the cell into two columns or into two rows. Be careful not to offset any of the business card layout.

5. Place your graphic as In Line with Text, preferably in its own cell within the single business card layout.

6. Place the text as desired.

7. Copy this one business card and paste it within the others.

8. Create one row of business cards.

9. Copy it and paste until you have five rows.

16. Notes, Bookmarks, Hyperlinks and Cross-References

These are tools that most people either rarely use or else they use them all the time. I cover the basics and answer some commonly asked questions.

These features are generally used to create manuals, school assignments and technical documents, but there are many other uses for the average user, too. You can use them to create a list of references or a bibliography.

Footnotes and Endnotes

When you create certain documents, you may need to refer to the source of the information therein. There is no difference, really, between a footnote and an endnote except in the placement.

> ➢ A footnote is placed at the bottom of the page on which the information appears.

> ➢ An endnote is placed at the end of the document in which the information appears.

Tip 33: Create a Footnote or Endnote

Generally, you'll place your insertion point just following the word, phrase, quote or paragraph for which you are providing a source reference.

1. Choose Insert→Footnote from Word's menu. Choose Footnote or Endnote, as desired.

2. Type the text of the footnote or endnote, which is generally a book or author name and/or other information about the source reference.

The Footnote and Endnote dialog box appears in Figure 16-1.

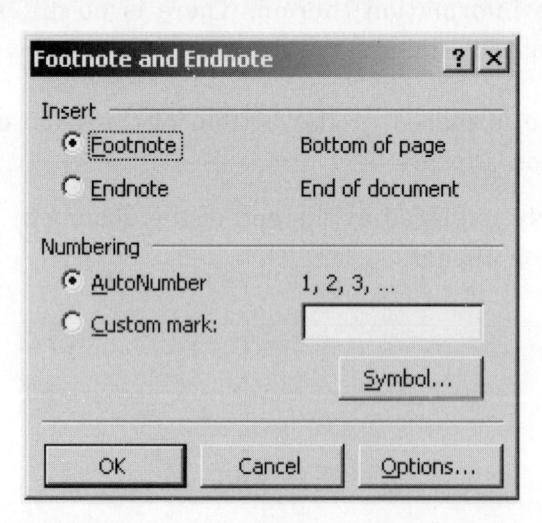

Figure 16-1: Footnote and Endnote Dialog Box

Formatting Footnotes and Endnotes

Many people don't like the single line that appears above footnotes. They either want to get rid of it or they want to make it thicker or longer.

Tip 34: Change a Footnote or Endnote Format

To change the appearance of the line or contents of a footnote at the bottom of the page, use these steps:

1. View→Normal
2. View→Footnotes
3. From the dropdown box, as shown in Figure 16-2, choose Footnote Separator.

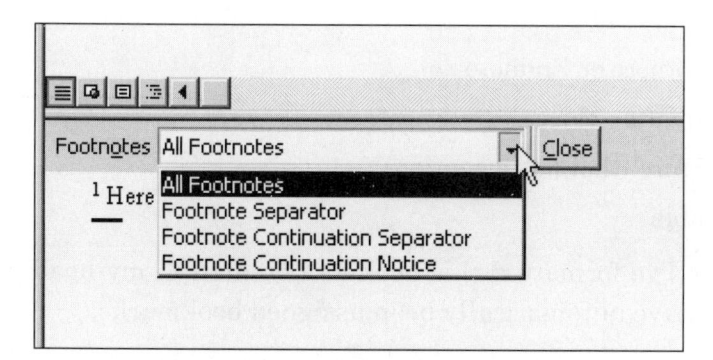

Figure 16-2: Change Footnote Formatting

4. Edit, Type, Delete as you would any other text and hit the Close button.

You can change the text formatting of a footnote or endnote by editing the Footnote or Endnote style as you would any other style. For information on changing style formatting, see page 9-7.

Dreamboat On Word   16-3

Bookmarks

Microsoft Word's Help defines a Bookmark as "an item or location in a document that you identify and name for future reference.

You can use bookmarks to quickly jump to a specific location, create cross-references, mark page ranges for index entries, and so on." They don't mention using bookmarks for hyperlinks, so I describe them below.

Automatic Bookmarks

Many bookmarks are automatically created; some are hidden and some are not. Using any of the following features, automatically creates a bookmark to that location:

- Heading styles
- Numbered or Outline numbered lists
- Form field
- Footnote or Endnote
- Equation object
- Figure (that has a caption)
- Table

Because I've formatted this book as I created it, my headings and figures have automatically been assigned bookmarks.

Cross-References

The main purpose of bookmarks is to create cross-references to them. Throughout this book, I have referred to different areas of the book for further information.

The perfect example is when I discuss a topic briefly and advise the reader to see more information that can be found on a certain page number. For instance, while that page number may be page 16-5 as I insert the cross-reference now, at the time of printing it may have become page Text Form Fields on page 18-5. So, instead, I inserted a cross-reference to the title of the *heading* Text Form Fields, in case I decide to change the heading name, and also to *page* 18-5, in case the page number changes as I continue to write my book.

One of the things I hate about cross-references can be found in on page 5-7. (Hmm...just used a bunch of cross-references there, did you catch them?)

You can create cross-references to any bookmark. Bookmark types are listed on page 16-4.

Hyperlinks

In order to create a hyperlink to an area of a Word document, the item must be bookmarked. See page 16-4 to learn about bookmarks. Once a bookmark is created, it's as simple as selecting the text or graphic in your document and then hitting Ctrl+K on your keyboard or the Insert Hyperlink button on your toolbar:

Figure 16-3: Insert Hyperlink Toolbar Button

There are several different types of hyperlink locations to which you can link:

- Existing File or Web Page
- Place in This document
- New Document
- Email Address

Depending on the type of hyperlink you choose to go to, the Insert→Hyperlink dialog box changes the objects from which you can choose. Figure 16-4 shows the Insert Hyperlink Dialog Box with Existing File or Web Page selected as the type.

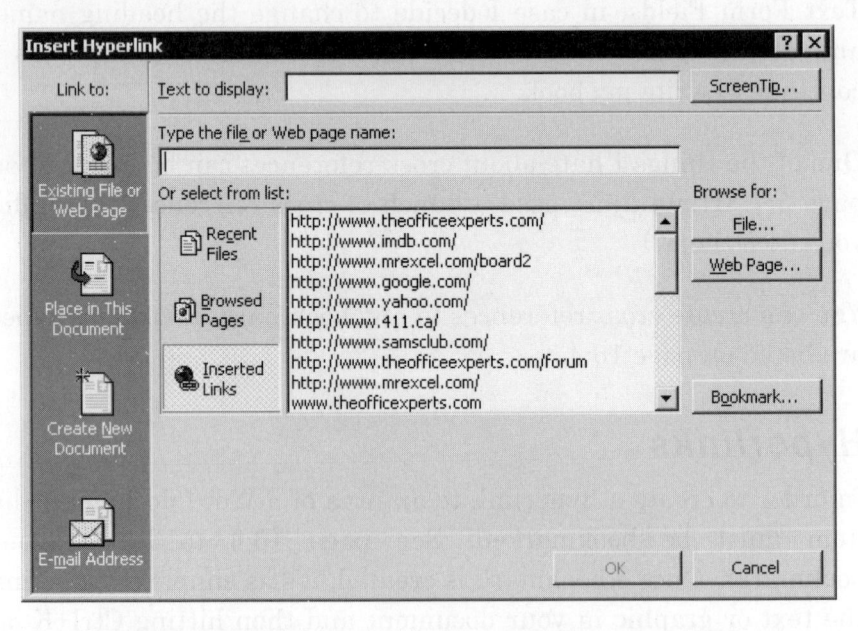

Figure 16-4: Insert Hyperlink Dialog Box (File or Web Page)

When Place in this Document is selected, you'll see a list of all of the bookmarks available in the document. Create new document allows you to create and save a new document to which you'd like to hyperlink. Email address creates a special hyperlink that launches your default email program with a message pre-addressed to the email address you've provided in the hyperlink.

Tip 35: Insert Hyperlinks to Other Document Types

Many people use the hyperlink command within the same kinds of documents but cannot figure out how to get from one type to the other. A classic example is trying to insert a hyperlink to an Excel file or vice-versa.

When you choose to Browse for a file, and choose an Excel File, no bookmarks appear like they do when you're trying to insert a hyperlink to a Word document. So, here's an example of how to do it:

Bookmarks don't exist in Excel, but named ranges do the same thing. If you have a named range called "MyPlace," simply insert a bookmark to the Excel file and type **#MyPlace** behind the rest of the bookmark so that it looks something like this:

C:\MyFiles\MyExcelFile.xls#MyPlace

Use the same method to insert a hyperlink in Excel to a Word bookmark, etc.

Notes, Bookmarks, Hyperlinks and Cross-References

Tip 36: Error "A security problem has occurred."

This can occur primarily on sites that begin with http**s**://

The "s" designates that it is a secure page. The URL must be in your history file (of previously visited sites) for Internet Explorer (IE) to allow you access to the site; IE does not allow you to open it for the first time through a hyperlink.

The only recourse is to use Visual Basic for Applications code in your file to intercept the link and open IE for you.

16-8   Dreamboat On Word

17. Mail Merge

Microsoft has done it again. They made a fairly nice tool, and then botched it up in the most recent version—Word 2002/XP.

The Mail Merge wizard was fairly easy to use. Now, with task panes, many of us just cannot figure out how to use it properly.

Main Documents

Mail merges are used when the same printed matter or email needs to be sent to multiple people. When you receive those prize-winning envelopes in the mail and wonder how it was typed "just for you," they have surely used a mail merge feature from some piece of software.

When you need to create labels for your holiday card list or a letter to let all your clients know that you're moving, mail merge is just the ticket.

Mail merges can also be used for other purposes. Suppose you keep track of all the personal computers at your company and you need to put a label on each one containing its specifications. You can create a data file containing that information (perhaps you already have a data file) and then create a mail merge that places the information in a standard format on a large label to place on each machine.

Using mail merge, you can easily create any number of products:

- Letters
- Mailing labels
- File folder labels
- Name tags
- Place setting tags
- Product tags

There are three documents for a mail merge: the final product or merged document that is created; the main document, or

Mail Merge

"boilerplate," from which the mail merge is performed; and the data source that is merged into the main document.

Data Sources

In versions prior to Word 2002/XP, the default data source that is created when you chose Create Data Source is a table in a Word document. This is reasonable because users who own only Word do not need any other application to create a mail merge.

One of the weird things about having a Word document as a data source is that if there are too many columns, the data table may not fit on your portrait layout document. You can make a custom page size of up to 22" by 22" in Word to overcome this limitation, or just copy your data table into Excel directly.

New in 2002/XP is that the default data source is now an Access database, which is, by default, stored in My Documents\My Data Sources.

Tip 37: Viewing the Mail Merge Toolbar (Word 2002/XP)

Word 2002/XP practically forces you to use the new Mail Merge Wizard in the task pane. So, if you simply want to edit or work in a merged document that you've already created, you'll first have to choose to view the mail merge toolbar by choosing it from the View→ Toolbars list.

One drawback has always been that new users of the Mail Merge feature have difficulty understanding that the data source is actually a separate file. Often, that separate file is much easier to edit than using the data entry form that Word provides for this purpose.

If you don't have a data source file already, then I strongly suggest using an Excel file for this purpose. Although many things can be done in Word, like sorting your lists, it just makes sense to use a program that handles data intuitively, such as Excel does.

An Access database works just as well as a data source, but many users are intimidated by Access. The basis for an Access database is the tables created within it. While there are more "rules" to creating tables in Access than there are in creating Excel files, you may want to look at those tables as simple Excel files for now—they're just in a new container. Hopefully this keeps a few of you from fearing the Access database default data source.

Using Queries

The ability to query your data source is a grossly under-used feature of Word's mail merge. Quite simply, you can ask for the mail merge to only merge to certain records. Suppose you are a small business trying to get your name out into your local community. You've set up a plan to send out three consecutive letters—one every three months. If your prospects haven't contacted you by then, you'll drop them from the list. Here's one way to accomplish your goal.

Scenario

You created a mail merge and sent your business card with it to introduce yourself to local companies.

In your data source, add a column named "First Letter" and enter the date that you sent the letter. Create another column called "Contacted Me" and put the date that any of the prospects

Mail Merge

contacted you. So, let's suppose you sent 100 letters and 5 of those people contacted you.

You really want to get a response from those other 95 people, so you create a mail merge to send a letter that has a 10%-Off coupon attached. (Because you've already got those five people interested, there's no need to send them the coupon.)

You'll want to use a mail merge query to create letters to send only to those 95 people who have not yet contacted you, so just prior to merging the documents, you must choose only those who have no date in the Contacted Me field.

Refer to Figure 17-1 on how to "query" the data sources for these values using Word 2002/XP.

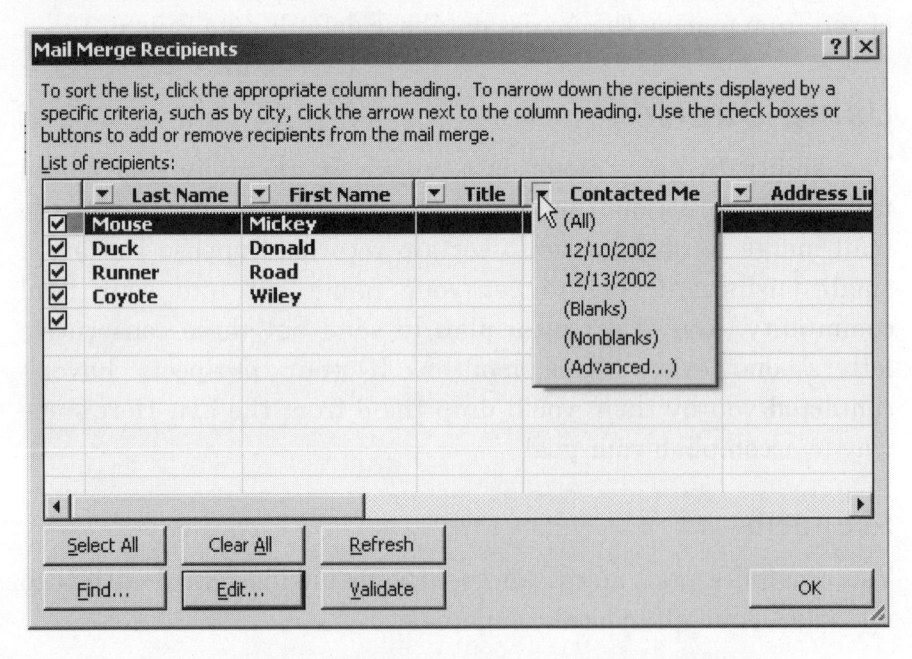

Figure 17-1: Word 2002/XP Mail Merge Recipients Dialog Box

Refer to Figure 17-2 on how to "query" the data sources for these values using Word 97/2000.

Mail Merge

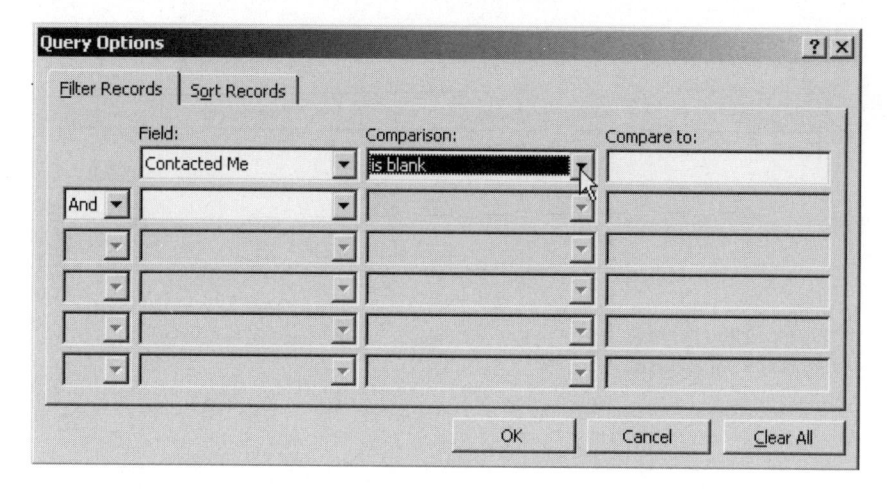

Figure 17-2: Word 97/2000 Query Options Dialog Box

Conditional Mail Merges

Don't confuse a conditional mail merge with a mail merge query. Though they can be similar, they are not the same.

Suppose you have a retail store with a men's department and a women's department. Your data source has a column for Gender and contains M for Male and F for Female.

If they're male, you want to have a sentence in your letter that reads:

> Visit our Men's Department today!

And, of course, if they're female, you want that sentence to read:

> Visit our Women's Department today!

Choose from the Mail Merge toolbar: Insert Word Field→ If...Then...Else... to get the dialog displayed in Figure 17-3.

Mail Merge

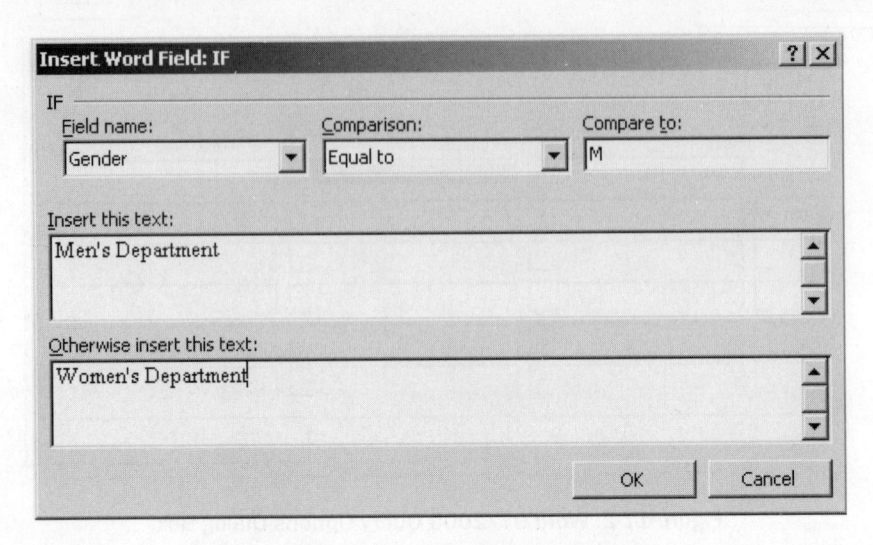

Figure 17-3: Insert Word field: IF Dialog Box

When you hit OK and turn your field codes to be viewable, it'll look like Figure 17-4.

{ IF { MERGEFIELD Gender } = "M" "Men's Department" "Women's Department" }

Figure 17-4: Mail Merge Conditional IF Statement

Tip 38: Show/Hide Field Codes

Make your field codes viewable by hitting the shortcut keys Alt+F9. Do the same to turn them off again. A lot of people see field codes accidentally, so you'll want to remember how to turn off viewing them.

Very detailed conditional statements can be written and there are people out there who can write them without help from the dialogs. I am not one of them. However, here are some tips that may help:

Mail Merge

> Begin by making sure that you're viewing codes (Alt+F9).

> Create a field by using Ctrl+F9 and begin typing your IF statement.

> Hit Ctrl+F9 again each time you need to insert additional bracket sets.

Tip 39: Correct Number and Date Formatting of Merge Fields

Make your field codes viewable by hitting the shortcut keys Alt+F9. Do the same to turn them off again. A lot of people see field codes accidentally, so you'll want to remember how to turn off viewing them.

It seems recent versions of Word have this problem more than older versions. You merge to a date field in Excel, and it's formatted improperly after you merge it.

If your merge fields aren't formatted right, you can force them. Two examples are shown in Figure 17-5.

{ MERGEFIELD Amount \# "0.00" }

{ MERGEFIELD Date \@ "mm/dd/yyyy" }

Figure 17-5: Mail Merge Field Format Statement

Dreamboat On Word   17-7

Mail Merge

Printing Mail Merge Documents

Sometimes your print job gets messed up. Now, perhaps, you need to reprint only one letter in your mail merge. How?

Tip 40: Print Only One Mail Merged Letter

Find the letter you want to print, which you can generally do by searching for the name or other unique information.

Note the section number at the bottom-left of the Word screen. In Figure 17-6, the section is "6."

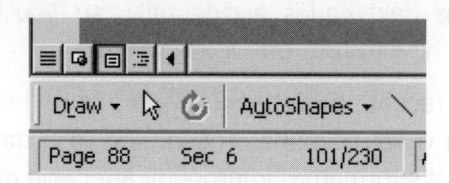

Figure 17-6: Word's Status Bar

Each letter in a merged Word document is its own section. So you'll only need to print section 6 in this case.

To do so, hit File→Print. In the Pages box (see Figure 17-7), type "S6" and hit Ok. If your merged documents are only one page in length, there's no need to note the section. Just find the letter, hit File→Print and choose Current Page.

For more on printing, see Printing and Printing Issues on page 20-1.

Mail Merge

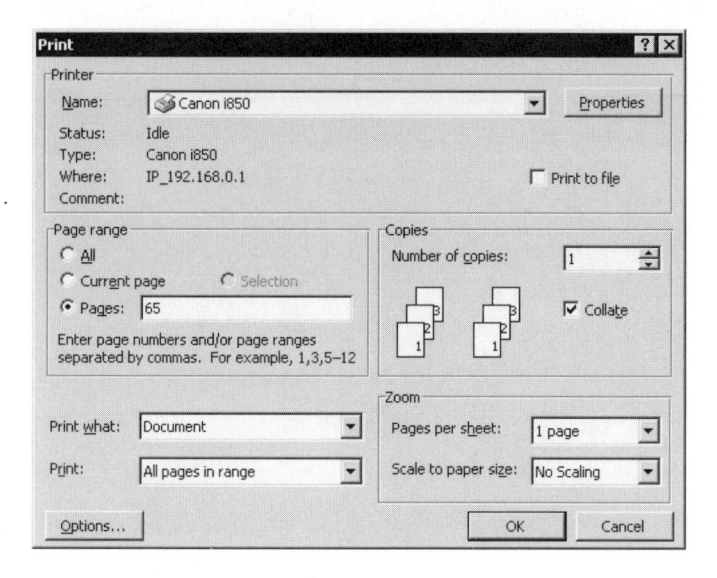

Figure 17-7: Word's Print Dialog

This page intentionally left blank.

18. Creating Forms

There are several kinds of "forms" in Microsoft Word. We'll review each type that does not require VBA coding.

Tip 41: Shading Form Fields

> To prepare your Word settings to work best with creating forms, go to Tools→Options, View tab and choose Field Shading [Always].

Macro Button Field Forms

When you open Word and hit File→New, you can choose one of Word's built-in templates. The graphic in Figure 18-1 was captured from the Contemporary Fax template.

TO:
[Click **here** and type name]

COMPANY:
[Click **here** and type company name]

FAX NUMBER:
[Click **here** and type fax number]

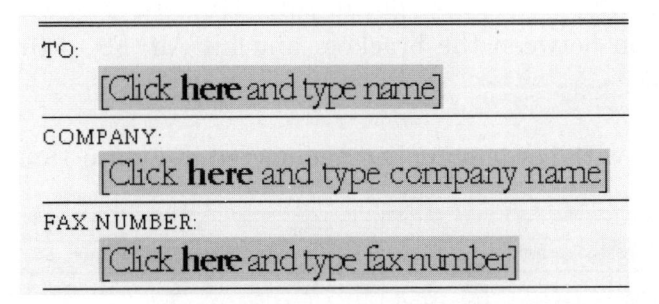

Figure 18-1: Macro Button Fields

There is no real mystery to creating this type of form. If you select the areas in which the fields reside and apply table borders, you see that it's nothing but a simple table, with macro buttons inserted into certain cells.

Dreamboat On Word   18-1

Creating Forms

There are no restrictions on these forms; they just help the user complete the form with the necessary information. Unlike protected, fill-in forms, these can also be edited and changed by the user in areas other than the form area.

When you view the code behind the form by hitting Alt+F9, it looks rather different:

TO:
{MACROBUTTON NoMacro [Click here and type name]}
COMPANY:
{MACROBUTTON NoMacro [Click here and type company name]}
FAX NUMBER:
{MACROBUTTON NoMacro [Click here and type fax number]}

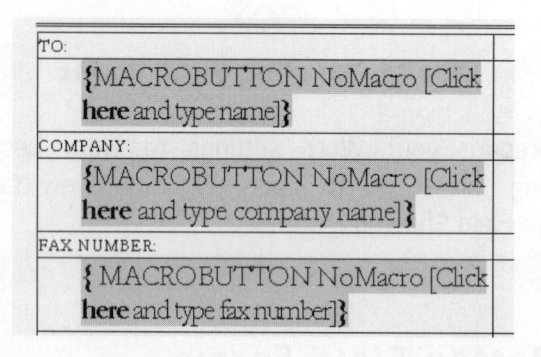

Figure 18-2: Macro Button Fields with Field Codes Revealed

Macro buttons are used here, but not with their original purpose. You can easily copy these fields from existing templates, and paste them into your document. Hit Alt+F9; change the instruction between the brackets and hit Alt+F9 to turn off the code view.

The table with borders applied is depicted in Figure 18-3.

TO:	FROM:
[Click here and type name]	[Click here and type name]
COMPANY:	DATE:
[Click here and type company name]	3/19/2003
FAX NUMBER:	TOTAL NO. OF PAGES INCLUDING COVER:
[Click here and type fax number]	[Click here and type number of pages]
PHONE NUMBER:	SENDER'S REFERENCE NUMBER:
[Click here and type phone number]	[Click here and type reference number]
RE:	YOUR REFERENCE NUMBER:
[Click here and type subject of fax]	[Click here and type reference number]

Figure 18-3: Fax Template with Borders Applied

Tip 42: Creating Click & Type Fields

Choose Insert→Field, choose the category ALL and choose MacroButton from the field name list. If you're in Word 2002/XP, hit the Field Codes button first. You'll note that the syntax displayed is shown as:

MACROBUTTON MacroName DisplayText

In the Field Codes box, type in:

MACROBUTTON NoMacro [Click here to type]

"Click here to type" is the text you want to have the user see. The brackets are not required, but give a nice look to the clickable area.

When you're done creating all of the fields you need, you can save it as a template. Choose File-New and double-click your template whenever you want to use it.

Fill-In Forms

Fill-in forms are so misunderstood! They're one of the easiest things to create. What are they good for? How many times have you received a form to fill out, and then, when you type in the information, the underlines move over and your text isn't underlined anyway? It works great if you print it and fill it out by hand, but how do you get it back to the sender now? Well, you could scan it with a scanner, but why did they send you this kind of form anyway?

Although the directions seem lengthy, they're quick to learn, and you can master them easily.

Open the Forms toolbar by choosing View→Toolbars→Forms. The toolbar looks like Figure 18-4, which shows the Word 2002/XP Forms Toolbar.

Figure 18-4: Word 2002/XP Forms Toolbar

Form Fields

Form fields are the area in your document where your user will be able to enter information. When your form is complete, the fields are the ONLY areas of the document that can be changed.

Text Form Fields

Click on the ab| button to insert a text form field. Double-click the gray form field that appears, or click on the form field and hit the Properties button (the icon with the hand on it) on the Forms toolbar. You now have a Properties window for that text form field. Refer to Figure 18-5.

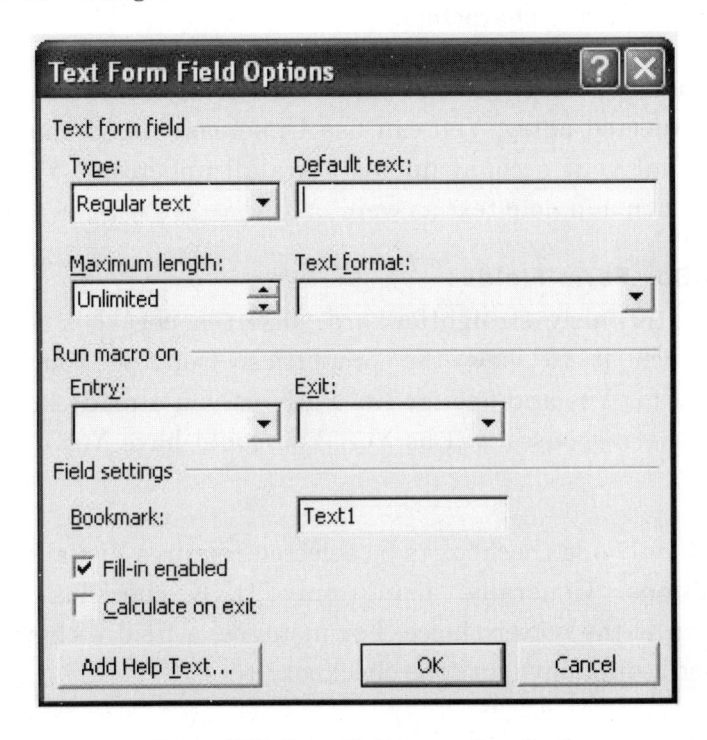

Figure 18-5: Form Field Properties - Text

Suppose that you are creating a contract form and this particular field will be used for the contractor's name. Give this form field a bookmark name of "Contractor." Bookmarks can only be one word, so if you use "Contractor Name," you must put "ContractorName" or "Contractor_Name" as the bookmark.

By giving the bookmark a name you understand, it's easy to later insert cross-references to the bookmark in your document.

Inserting a cross-reference makes the same information appear again, without having to type it again.

Suppose you want to use this text form field for an account number and suppose that your account numbers are something like ABC01, ABC02, etc. You will want to restrict the size of this text form field to 5 characters.

As the default value, you can enter LLLNN to indicate the syntax of the expected entry. You can use Uppercase text formatting to ensure that your account numbers are all uppercase. You'll note that you can add help text as well.

Check Box Form Fields

This one is fairly straightforward. Insert a checkbox and then double-click it to view the properties. Suppose you have a checkbox for Yes and one for No. Perhaps you already know that 60% of the responses will be Yes. You could have Yes default to checked.

To allow only one checkbox to be selected requires Visual Basic for Applications. Generally, using only ONE checkbox for the exception is the better choice. For instance, a field with the label "Married" could have just one checkbox.

Dropdown Form Fields

These form fields are much easier than you would think! Insert one and double-click it. You can add items to the list and organize them alphabetically or from the most popular to least popular. A field like this can be used for choosing from a list of specific items. This avoids mistakes from typos, particularly if your list is limited.

There's a 25-item limit! If you find yourself needing more, label each drop-down form field with some kind of criteria. For instance, suppose you've got 73 department names. Make three drop-down form fields, one each for department names that begin with A through J, K through R, and S through Z. The only other alternative is a Visual Basic for Applications object combo box.

Consider using the drop-down form field instead if, for instance, you have a limited number of accounts as described under the Text form field options.

If you do not want your drop-down form field to appear as if the first item is selected, create an item using a dozen or so spaces. Even though you cannot see it, you can move it to the top of the list in the properties box. When the form is viewed, that item shows nothing selected. You could also put a choice called "Choose from List."

Creating Forms in Tables

If your form is, for instance, a subcontractor agreement that is fairly standard, you will just want to insert form fields as described above.

However, if your form is something that needs to mostly be completed by the user, you may want to use tables. Forms with tables are especially nice because they can be filled out electronically and by hand. Using table borders to underline your form field can make it look like it was a form that was put into a typewriter and completed.

Suppose you need name and date on one line. Make four columns. The first cell should contain "Name:,", the second should contain your form field and have a bottom border on it (unless you are keeping all of your cell borders). The third should contain "Date:,", and the fourth should contain a text form field formatted as a date and can have a bottom border. The following Tip describes how to accomplish your goal.

Creating Forms

Tip 43: Creating Forms in Tables

Some of these instructions can apply to Macrobutton forms too.

Begin by turning on the Forms toolbar. Then create a table that has twice as many columns as it does entries (check box form fields only require one column).

With the Show/Hide button on, the form might look something like Figure 18-6 while you develop it.

Name	°°°°°	Date	°°°°°
Address	°°°°°	Course	Choose ±
City, State, Zip	°°°°°	Phone	°°°°°

Figure 18-6: Sample Form—Developer View

You can also change the sizes of the cells to get the most out of your available space, as shown in Figure 18-7.

Name		Date	
Address		Course	Choose
City, State, Zip		Phone	

Figure 18-7: Sample Form with Resized Cells

Dreamboat On Word

Creating Forms

When you've completed the form, you can remove certain borders from the table, if desired, which gives you something like Figure 18-8.

Name		Date	
Address		Course	Choose
City, State, Zip		Phone	

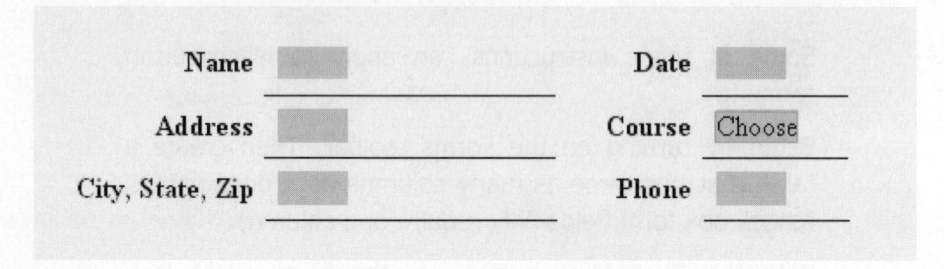

Figure 18-8: Sample Form—User View

Protecting Fill-In Forms

These types of form documents must be protected for the form fields to work. The last button on the Forms toolbar, which looks like a padlock, allows you to quickly protect the form while you are creating it to ensure that your form fields work as planned. However, to truly protect your form prior to actually using it, go to Tools→Protect Document and choose Forms. Give it a password if you like.

Tip 44: Cautions on Protecting Forms

Warning: When you protect the form, fill it out and then decide to change something in the form, you must unprotect it. If you unprotect it, fix that item, then re-protect your form, all of your filled-in form fields will be empty again!

New in Word 2002/XP: This behavior does not occur; the fields are not reset to be blank.

Warning: You may have protected your form, but anyone can create a new document from it simply by opening a blank document, hitting Insert→File and inserting your form document. Your form is now unprotected, whether you used a password to protect the original or not. The good thing is that if you forget the password for your form, you can use the same method to unprotect it and then re-protect it.

Spell checking Protected Fill-In Forms

After completing your form, your users may want to spell check it. The spell check option is grayed-out and unavailable. The form must be unprotected, spell checked and then re-protected. You will not want to let your users do this because they may lose the entries they've made. Visual Basic for Applications code is required to work around this in versions 2000 and below.

Tip 45: Creating Hyperlinks in Protected Forms

Hyperlinks don't Work in Protected Forms? That's right. So here's your workaround:

1. You will need to have a form field to which you want to hyperlink or you can create one. (If you want this to be a *hidden* form field, particularly if you are protecting your document but not for form purposes, select it and make it one point in font size and one character in length.)

2. Give the bookmark a friendly name for you to refer to.

3. Record a macro that does an Edit-Go To to the bookmark for that form field.

4. Insert a command button next to what you would have clicked on for your hyperlink.

5. Have that command button run your macro.

User Forms

User forms are created using Visual Basic for Applications code. I felt no reason to reinvent the wheel and Malcolm Smith has a great tutorial on creating a template with a userform under his Tutorials section at www.dragondrop.com.

19. Drawing in Word

The Drawing toolbar with its tools and WordArt are available for use in almost all of the Office applications (not available in Outlook). As I discuss them here, I refer to their use only from a Word point-of-view and not of their use in other applications.

Office Drawing Tools

With Word 2002/XP, using the drawing tools isn't half as much fun as it used to be. They've given us something called a Drawing Canvas and many don't like it. Well, you don't have to use it. Just go to Tools→Options. On the General tab, simply uncheck the last checkbox marked "Automatically create drawing canvas…"

It's been my experience that documents that contain Office drawing tools have a tendency to become corrupt more often than ones that do not contain them. I suspect it is due to Word not being able to keep track of many individual drawing objects at once. While I don't have enough personal use or experience with documents that are created in Word 2002/XP and used only in that version, I suspect the issue remains because I see this problem as much as ever.

Tip 46: Working With Office Drawing Objects

This tip applies to using the Office Drawing Tools in any application. If your drawing contains more than a couple objects, or if you file contains more than several graphics creating using the Drawing toolbar, then you may want to follow these suggested steps:

1. Create your drawings in another Word document.
2. Select all of the objects they've used in their drawing and group them.
3. Save the Word document for use later—as you would a graphic file.
4. Copy the drawing.
5. In the actual document you want the drawing to be in, hit Edit→Paste Special, as a Picture. (Enhanced metafile appears to provide the best image.)

WordArt

First of all, may I say that if you want your document to be professional, don't use WordArt. It's a terrific feature for an in-house newsletter, a social club flyer or other non-business-related materials, but it doesn't belong in a professional setting. You should not create your company logo with it.

There are many other graphic programs available for little or no money that provide much better features than WordArt.

If you want to learn WordArt, go for it. It's very simple to use and doesn't require any special skills. Of course, you should play with it. To my knowledge, its only true redeeming quality is the ability to "arc" or "wave" text.

PhotoDraw

Microsoft Office 2000 Premium came with a program called PhotoDraw. This is one of the best programs ever created. Microsoft has discontinued it. I suspect that I'll be using it for a long time. Few people seem to be aware of its existence.

If you have Office 2000 Premium, look for PhotoDraw and use it! You can get some of the effects you've always wanted without a cumbersome and expensive professional graphics program like CorelDraw or Adobe PhotoShop.

Graphics and Drawing Tips

You can easily access the Drawing toolbar by choosing the Drawing toolbar button on the Standard toolbar (refer to Figure 19-1), or by View→Toolbars and choose Drawing.

Figure 19-1: Drawing Toolbar On/Off Toggle Button

> ➤ Keep your file sizes to a minimum by inserting your graphics and then converting them to pictures. This does not apply to objects created from the drawing toolbar and should be tested in a copy of the file to ensure that it helps because it doesn't always.

Drawing in Word

- Try this in a file that you feel is oversized for its content:
    1. Save a copy of the file to another name.
    2. Select each graphic or picture.
    3. Cut it.
    4. Hit Edit→Paste Special and choose As a Picture (Enhanced metafile option is best if it's available).
    5. Do this to at least 25% of the graphics in your document. Save the file and check the new file size. For the most part, it should be smaller than the original. Sometimes, it is significantly smaller. This entire manual, complete with embedded graphics, is less than 2MB.

- Keep your file sizes to a minimum by inserting your graphics as links. If your graphics are separate files, try linking instead of embedding them. While a document with all the graphics embedded might be 50MB, the document and graphics separately ought to be about the same size.

    The benefit is that the PC, when opening the document, doesn't need to have enough RAM to open a 50MB file all at once; it only needs enough for the size of the document and the graphic(s) currently being viewed.

    Also, you can send the files via email in several pieces that total 50MB instead of one big 50MB file. Another benefit is that if you edit one of the graphics, you don't need to change the document. The document simply picks up the edited graphic.

- If you want to add callouts, arrows or other drawing objects to a graphic, that graphic must not be formatted as In Line With Text. There is no comparable description in Word 97 for this; it is simply the opposite of Float Over Text.

    However, after adding the drawn objects, you can select them along with the graphic and group them using Draw→Group from the Drawing toolbar. Then, you can cut it and hit

Edit→Paste Special, As a Picture, which allows the In Line With Text option to become available.

- Do not be surprised if the rotation tool is not available when you select your graphic or drawn object because most drawing objects and graphics cannot be rotated. You can cut the object, paste it into Paint or some other graphic program, and rotate it there.

- Text wrapping around graphics can be difficult. If you cannot make the text wrapping work as desired, try inserting a one-row, two-column table. Put your text in one cell and your graphic in the other.

- When creating watermarks or other graphics on every page, place the graphic in the header. This helps keep you from accidentally selecting the graphic while you work in your document.

Graphics Layout Settings

Others may disagree with me, but I strongly suggest that you use "In line with text" as your default graphic placement. Choose Format→Picture or double-click the picture to bring up the Format Picture dialog box shown in Figure 19-2.

Drawing in Word

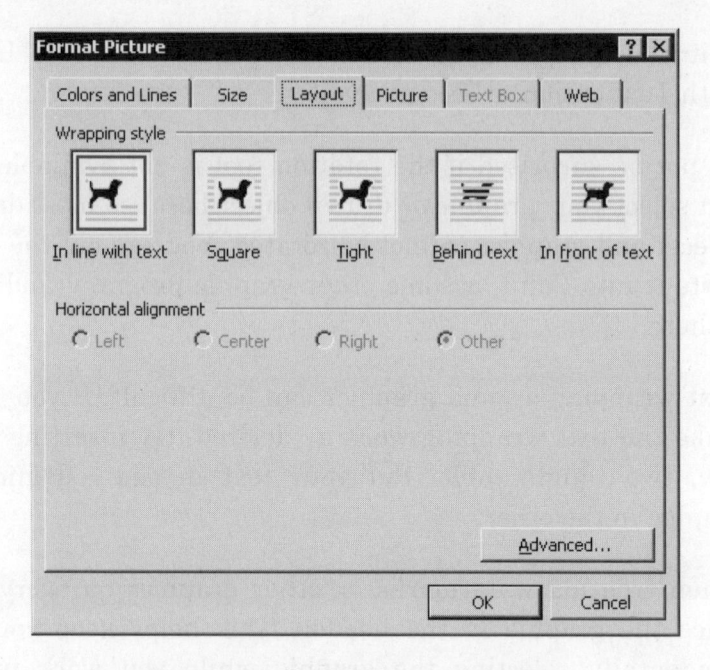

Figure 19-2: Format Picture Dialog Box

In line with text

Use this for most purposes and especially when graphics are placed inside of table cells.

Tip 47: Place Graphics In Line With Text

The different Wrapping styles provide different results. By choosing In line with text, you can position your graphic the same way that you would a paragraph of text. Best of all, you can create a style for graphics in your document.

When laying out this book, I created a style called Graphic, which has 18 points before and 12 points after the graphic; the graphic is centered and is formatted as Keep with Next so that I don't find my graphic at the bottom of one page and its caption at the top of the next.

The drawback is that you cannot position your graphic anywhere; you can only position it as you would some paragraph text.

When selected, a graphic that is formatted as Inline with text gets a black border and black resizing handles as shown in Figure 19-3. This method does NOT allow you to drag your graphic around the page.

Figure 19-3: Selected Graphic Formatted as Inline with Text

Square & Tight

Use these wrapping styles for small pictures in newsletters or in a flyer.

Behind Text

Use this wrapping style for watermarks, background graphics and similar tasks.

In Front of Text

Rarely used except for artistic purposes, such as creating a CD-Rom label, manual cover or other artistic product.

Graphics that are formatted with Square, Tight, Behind text or In front of text look like the graphic in Figure 19-4. When formatted this way, the graphic can easily be dragged around to any location on the page.

The Office Experts

Figure 19-4: Selected Graphic That is NOT Inline with Text

Float Over Text

Word 97 does not have all of these layout options, and objects are either placed as "float over text" or they are not, which would be referred to as inline with text.

A picture that is formatted to float over text in Word 97 appears as shown in Figure 19-5 when selected.

The Office Experts

Figure 19-5: Selected Graphic Formatted as Float Over Text

20. Printing and Printing Issues

There are many printing issues with Word. Many have been around for years without being dealt with by Microsoft. It's difficult to blame them, however, because it must be very difficult to accommodate all the different printers available and all of the different page layouts.

Printing Page Ranges

Suppose you have a 100-page document and each chapter starts renumbering with page 1. You want to print the 88th page of the 6th chapter. Instead of printing page 101, as shown in the Status Bar in Figure 20-1, you'll want to print Section 6, Page 88. To do this, you simply type p88s6 into the Pages box.

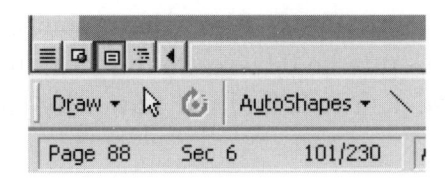

Figure 20-1: Word's Status Bar

Figure 20-2 shows the Print dialog box.

Printing and Printing Issues

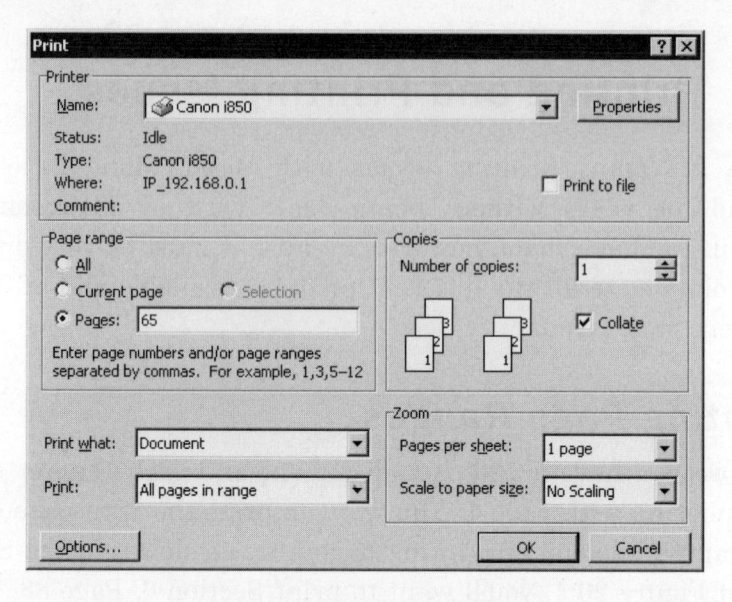

Figure 20-2: Word's Print Dialog

I've occasionally come across files where someone numbers the first page of a section to be 0 (zero) so that they'll have the second page read as page 1. You'll find out now why this is not a good practice.

You can print specific pages using several different formats. Here are a few examples:

Cod s	Print Results
s1-p1s2	Section 1 in its entirety and Page 1 only of Section 2.
s1,s2,s4	Sections 1, 2 and 4
s1-s4	Sections 1 through 4
s1,s4	Section 1 and Section 4
p1s1-p4s1,p5s2	Pages 1 through 4 of Section 1, and Page 5 of Section 2. Note that if the first page of Section 2 is not numbered "1," your results could vary.

To really understand the behavior of the print range codes, you can try this little exercise:

Tip 48: Understanding Print Range Codes

Printing only certain ranges of multi-section documents can be quickly understood by following these steps:

1. Create a document with multiple sections and multiple pages in each section.
2. Set up page numbering any way you like.
3. On each page, type the exact page number and section number that are shown in the status bar.
4. Using the table above, try printing several different ranges.

Blank Pages

Blank pages can occur for several reasons. Blank pages can appear throughout the document or at the end of the document.

At the Bottom/End of the Document

This generally occurs because you've got non-printing characters at the bottom of your document.

Method 1 Fix: Deleting Unnecessary Characters
1. Turn your Show/Hide button on.
2. Hit View and choose either Print Layout or Page Layout.
3. Hit Ctrl+End.
4. Backspace until all non-printing characters have been deleted.

Method 2 Fix: For Documents with Tables Only

If you have a table on your first page and cannot remove that last paragraph that is the only thing on the next page, select that paragraph return and change the font size to 1. You cannot select font size 1; you must type it into the font size box and hit Enter.

Throughout the Document

Different printers may need more space at the bottom of the sheet of paper to allow the rollers to pull the paper through the printer. Rule of thumb: the less you paid for your printer, the more of the paper it uses for rolling. Thus, if you set your document up for a printer that allows a 0.5" margin at the bottom, and then take it to another PC that is connected only to a printer that requires a 0.6" margin at the bottom, you may end up with extra pages because the page breaks (manual or automatic) now break "sooner."

Tip 49: Minimum Margins for Your Printer

Here's how to determine the minimum margins for your printer:

1. Open a blank document.

2. Set all margins to zero and hit OK. You should be told that your margins are outside of the printable area and should choose to Fix or Ignore it.

3. Choose FIX.

4. Go back into the margins and see what they have been changed to. These are the minimum margins of which your printer is capable. You may want to set your Word default margins to be at least as large as the minimums.

For best results, determine the minimum margins you'll use for all documents. I like to use 1.0" margins all the way around.

To change Word's default margins for your computer, hit File→Page Setup, choose the Margins tab. Change your margins and hit the DEFAULT button at the lower-left of the dialog. This will NOT change existing documents, only new ones.

Text Prints with Extra Space Between Letters or Words

Generally, the text doesn't appear badly while you're creating the document; only when you preview or print it.

This is a definite printer driver issue. Be sure you have the right printer driver for your printer and operating system.

Page Borders Don't Print

This occurs because not all printers are capable of printing so close to the bottom of the paper. See Page Borders on page 11-2.

This page intentionally left blank.

21. Macros and VBA

I don't intend to teach you Visual Basic for Applications in this book. However, if you become a little bit familiar with what macros are and learn your way around the Visual Basic Editor window, perhaps it'll spark your interest in automating your tasks. I figure if you're lazy, you'll LOVE macros!

What is a Macro?

Macros are used to create a set of commands or tasks to be performed automatically. When you have repetitive tasks, you can create a macro that automatically runs a small "program" to perform those tasks for you.

Visual Basic for Applications (VBA) is a mini-version of Visual Basic that is used within the Microsoft Office suite and certain other programs, like Visio. When you record a macro, the VBA code required to repeat those steps is recorded for you. Many tasks that you would like to perform cannot be recorded, but may be written in VBA; many tasks that you would like to perform all at once might need to be written by a VBA programmer.

Macro Security

Macros and VBA are one of the most misunderstood features of Word. The macro virus warning pop-up can still shock a seasoned user into cardiac arrest! The plain truth is that once you read this, you will no longer fear the warning; in fact, you should welcome it.

Tip 50: Avoiding Viruses

To avoid getting any type of virus into your system or company network:

- Never open emails from people that you don't know.
- Especially, never open email attachments from people you don't know.
- If in doubt, throw it out.
- If you open a Word document and receive the warning, ask the person who created it why you might be getting that warning before you enable macros.
- If you open a Word document that you created and no one has had access to it, immediately disable macros.

Although many companies set restrictions on your ability to run macros, most do not. Most companies leave this decision up to the user—as well they should. Keeping users from learning about macros (and macro security, of course) might as well be saying, "Now, now. We don't want you to become TOO efficient!"

So, if you are a decision maker about such things, we encourage you to distribute information about macros, macro security and encourage your users to use macros!

Tip 51: Setting Macro Security

For most users, being asked to enable macros when you open a document that contains macros is the best option. This always provides you with a choice.

To enable macros:

Version	Commands
Word 97	Tools→Options, General tab.
	☑ Macro virus protection
Word 2000	Tools→Macro→Security.
	⦿ Medium. You can choose whether or not to run potentially unsafe macros.
Word 2002/XP	You can access the setting the same as you can in 2000, however, there is an additional setting to consider. Click on the Trusted Sources tab and check the box shown below.
	☑ Trust all installed add-ins and templates
	This additional setting provides even stricter macro security. Checking it enables you to use the code in any add-ins or templates that you use.

For all of the macro security settings, use them at your own risk. There is absolutely no system completely invulnerable to viruses, however, and it is often fairly simple to clean a system of them.

Macros and VBA

I need to tell this story: Macro viruses were, for several years, nothing more than a nuisance. As insane as it sounds, there was a Word macro virus out there that I just loved. It would grab your user name from your PC and put some text behind it. Here's a message similar to what you'd get when you closed the file:

```
┌─ Microsoft Word ──────── X ─┐
│                             │
│  John Smith is a big stupid jerk! │
│                             │
│         ┌─────┐             │
│         │ OK  │             │
│         └─────┘             │
└─────────────────────────────┘
```

Figure 21-1: Macro Virus Message

While providing over-the-phone software support, there was nothing funnier than having some guy call and try to explain this problem. I remember one in particular. I could just tell this was an older gentleman and probably in an important position because he had his assistant put the call through. It was very tough not to giggle. Thank goodness, it's very easy to get rid of!

This macro "virus" is so ridiculously easy to create. Though I only suggest doing it to someone who can take a joke. See the section on page 21-15 to see how it's done.

Tip 52: Getting Rid of a Macro Virus

This method only gets rid of the simplest of macro viruses in Word. While we may call them viruses, they're generally just a piece of VB code that runs when you open, close, save or take some other action in your document(s).

On opening the infected file, the code tells your PC to copy the infecting code into your normal.dot file, thus it affects all files on your system, BUT IT DOES NOT INFECT THE FILES. This is a common belief that just isn't true.

You'll likely be able to pinpoint the infected file and clean it up yourself with the instructions in Clean Documents of Code, below. To clean your normal.dot, refer to Step 3 of Troubleshooting Word on page 24-9.

Clean Documents of Code

Yes, you can easily erase code from a document. I provide a sample macro that can clean all code out of a document on page 21-17. However, I thought we should introduce you to the Visual Basic Editor.

First ensure that the document should not contain any code and then follow these steps:

1. Open the VB Editor window (commonly referred to as the VBE) by using Alt+F11.

    You'll see the Project Explorer, as shown in Figure 21-2, in the upper, left-hand side of the window. If you don't see it, hit Ctrl+R.

Macros and VBA

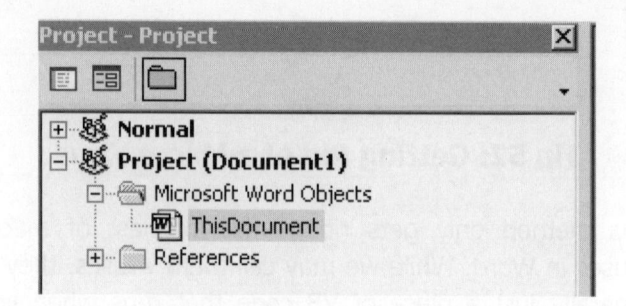

Figure 21-2: VBE Project Explorer

2. Double-click the ThisDocument object. On the right-hand side of the window, you'll see the Code window, as shown in Figure 21-3.

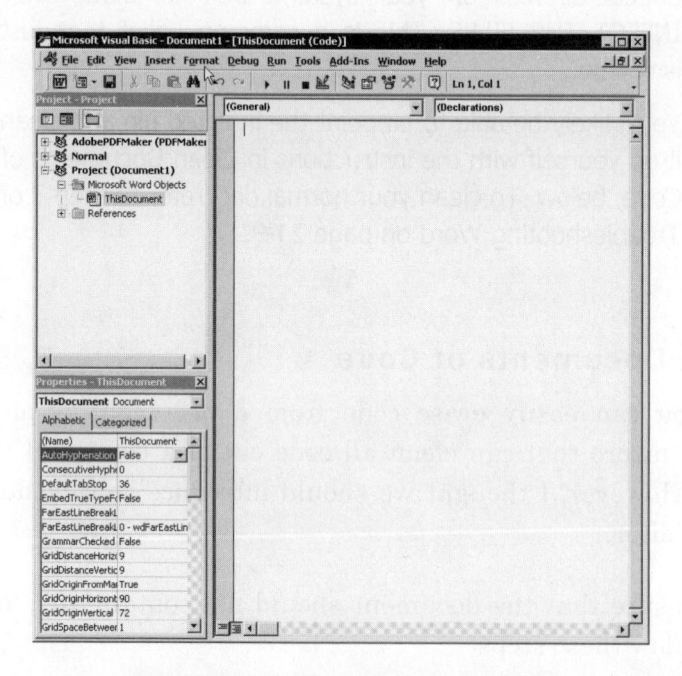

Figure 21-3: The Visual Basic Editor (VBE)

3. If you see any code in the Code window, click inside the code window, hit Ctrl+A to select all and hit your delete key.

There may or may not be code in ThisDocument or in any Module(s). The existence of a module, whether it contains code or not, fires the macro virus warning message on opening of the document if your Macro security is set to warn you.

If your Project Explorer looks like the one in Figure 21-4, you may then need to double-click the Module and do the same to delete the code from the code window as you did in Step 3, above.

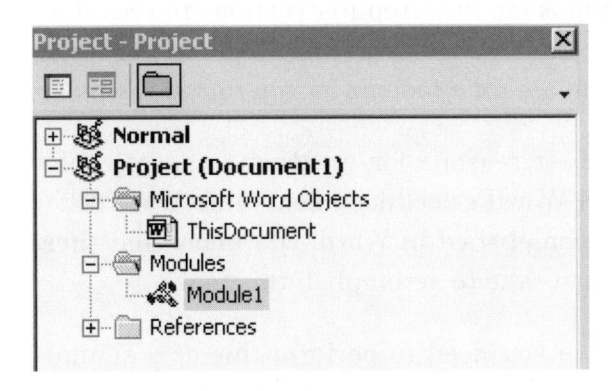

Figure 21-4: VBE Project Explorer with Modules

If any modules are empty, or if you have deleted the code from them, you can right-click each one and choose to Remove it. When asked if you'd like to export it before removing it, you likely want to choose not to do so.

However, if you have a piece of VB code in a Word file and you want to use it in another file, you can export a module and import it into another document.

Not all modules are named "Module." You may find that someone has renamed it to, for instance, "MrgModule," if they intended to place the code in the file for mail merge use. The name of modules is entirely up to the person who programs it.

How to Record a Macro

Recording macros in Word, Excel and PowerPoint becomes easy once you know how. Access and Outlook do not allow recording macros. They must be programmed.

The following is step-by-step instructions to record a macro, make the macro available for use in any single file or for use in any file you open, and assign a toolbar button to run the macro.

One of the best reasons for creating a macro could be that you must convert WordPerfect documents into Word documents. If you are fairly accomplished in Word, you know that there are several steps you must take to accomplish this task.

The next time you need to perform this or a similar task, record the tasks as a macro and you will only have to press a button to perform them again.

Step 1: Prepare to Record

If you would like the macro to be available in a specific file, open that file. If you would like the macro to be available in all files, create a new, blank document.

1. From the menu, hit Tools→ Macro→Record New Macro. The dialog box in Figure 21-5 appears:

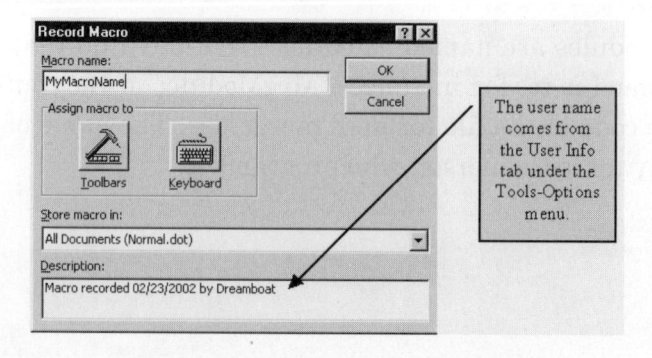

Figure 21-5: Record Macro Dialog Box

2. In the Macro name box, enter the name you would like to use for your macro. It must not have any spaces and should not contain special characters.

3. Decide where to store the macro. If you would like it available in the current document only, hit the Store Macro in dropdown box and select your active document's name. If you would like the macro to be available for use with any file, select All Documents (normal.dot).

4. Give the macro any description you like in the Description box. By default, the description states the date the macro was recorded and the user name, which automatically comes from the information under Word's Tools→ Options, User Info tab.

Step 2: Assign the Macro to a Toolbar Button

1. Click on the Toolbar icon to assign the macro to a toolbar button. If the macro name is invalid, you receive an error message and must rename the macro before you can continue. Figure 21-6 shows the dialog box that appears.

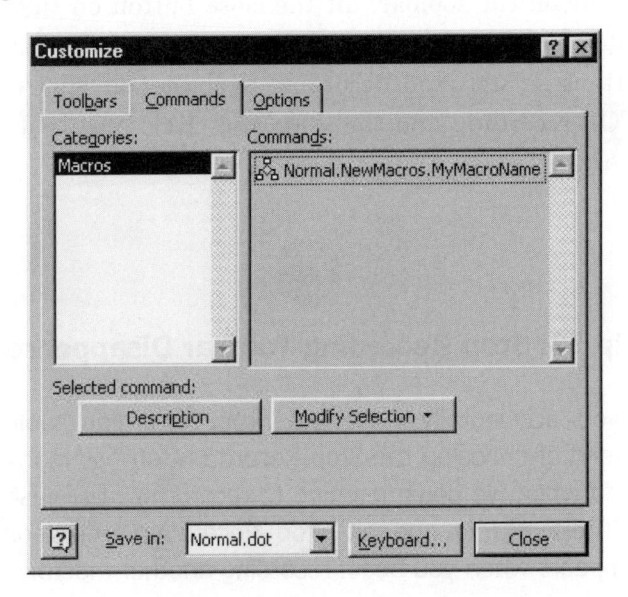

Figure 21-6: Customize Dialog Box

Macros and VBA

2. The Commands tab is selected by default. In the right column, there is an icon with a title similar to your macro's name. Click on the icon and drag it up to any location you choose on any toolbar you choose. Your mouse pointer must have a + hanging on it before you lift your finger from the mouse or the icon will not be placed. While dragging, you see an x hanging on your mouse pointer.

Figure 21-7 shows the different mouse pointers.

Figure 21-7: Customize Mouse Pointers

3. Once your icon is placed on a toolbar, click the Modify Selection button; various options appear. Refer to page 3-9 for further information on how to customize your toolbars.

4. When the button appears exactly as you would like it to appear on the toolbar, hit the close button on the Customize dialog box. The Stop Recording toolbar appears. There are two buttons on the Stop Recording toolbar. The square is used to STOP recording and the lines and circle are used to PAUSE recording.

Tip 53: Stop Recording Toolbar Disappeared

If you accidentally close the Stop Recording toolbar, instead of choosing the Stop Record button—as many of us do when we begin learning to record macros—just go to Tools→Macro and hit Stop Recording. The toolbar reappears when you begin recording another macro.

Step 3: Record the Macro

1. Perform the tasks you would like your new macro to perform for you.

2. If you need to interrupt the macro recording to perform some non-related work, press the Pause button on the Stop Recording toolbar.

3. Press the Pause button again to continue recording.

4. Hit the Stop button to Stop recording when you have finished recording your tasks.

Step 4: Test the Macro

Always test a macro, particularly if you have created it to run for someone else. To test the macro, click on the toolbar button you've created, or hit Tools→Macro→Macros and double-click the macro name.

Sample Word Macros

I'm providing several Word macros to give you an idea of the kind of automation that can be performed using VBA.

We have provided the code so that it is easy for you to type it. Whenever you see the ¶ symbol, it means you should hit Enter to create a paragraph return. Otherwise, you should not hit return while typing the code provided.

Some or all of these samples may be found in downloadable files on our website at www.TheOfficeExperts.com under the VBA Samples page.

Lines of code that begin with an apostrophe are comments and do not need to be typed into your code at all.

Sample Macro 1: Return Labels to Data

Many people create mail merge data sources in Word and then never save their data file, or are even unaware that it existed. This code is lengthy, but well worth typing.

Scenario

Suzy is to collect from each salesperson their lists of clients for sending holiday cards. She needs to combine the lists because it needs to be sorted in Zip Code order.

John sends a Word file full of labels to Suzy with a note that states, "Here's my list from last year."

Suzy wonders how she's going to integrate John's label-formatted addresses into the existing data list.

Solution

This macro is courtesy of my friend, Tom Giaquinto. After having manually converted many label files back to data source layouts, I can tell you that this macro can save you a great deal of time. This macro actually takes a mailing label-formatted document and converts it into a real data file, regardless of how many lines of text are on each label.

Questions on ways to perform this task quickly often come around the holidays when people are constructing holiday card mailing lists.

Type the following code into an inserted Module in your normal.dot and you'll be able to run the code on any Word document.

Code
```
Sub DataSorcerer()

  Dim tbl As Table    'Table object
  Dim x As Integer, y As Integer   'Counters
  Dim intRows As Integer   'Total rows in table
```

```vba
   Dim intCols As Integer   'Total Columns in table
   Dim intGotVal As Integer   'Test for blank cells

   'Select Entire Document and replace all line breaks
   'with temporary place holder
   Selection.WholeStory
   With Selection.Find
      .Text = "^p"
      .Replacement.Text = "<REPLACEMENT>"
   End With
   Selection.Find.Execute Replace:=wdReplaceAll

   Selection.WholeStory
   With Selection.Find
      .Text = "^l"
      .Replacement.Text = "<REPLACEMENT>"
   End With
   Selection.Find.Execute Replace:=wdReplaceAll

  'Convert all tables to text w/ paragraph symbols
   'used as delimiters
   For Each tbl In ActiveDocument.Tables
      tbl.Select
      tbl.Rows.ConvertToText
Separator:=wdSeparateByParagraphs
   Next tbl

   'Remove all section breaks from document
   Selection.WholeStory
   With Selection.Find
      .Text = "^b"
      .Replacement.Text = "^p"
   End With
   Selection.Find.Execute Replace:=wdReplaceAll

   'Replace all double line breaks w/ single line breaks
   Selection.WholeStory
   With Selection.Find
      .Text = "^p^p"
      .Replacement.Text = "^p"
   End With
   Selection.Find.Execute Replace:=wdReplaceAll

   'Replace temporary place holder w/ tabs to be used
   'when text is converted to table
   Selection.WholeStory
   With Selection.Find
```

Macros and VBA

```
      .Text = "<REPLACEMENT>"
      .Replacement.Text = "^t"
   End With
   Selection.Find.Execute Replace:=wdReplaceAll

   'Select entire document then convert to table w/ tabs
   'as delimiter
   Selection.WholeStory
   Selection.ConvertToTable Separator:=wdSeparateByTabs

   'Count rows and columns and set current table object
   intRows = ActiveDocument.Tables(1).Rows.Count
   intCols = ActiveDocument.Tables(1).Columns.Count
   Set tbl = ActiveDocument.Tables(1)

'Check for and remove blank rows
   For x = 1 To intRows
      intGotVal = 0
      For y = 1 To intCols
         If tbl.Cell(x, y).Range.Characters.Count > 1 Then
            intGotVal = intGotVal + 1
             y = intCols
         Else
            'Do Nothing
         End If
      Next y

      If intGotVal = 0 Then
         tbl.Rows(x).Delete
         x = x - 1
      Else
         'Do Nothing
      End If
   Next x

   'Check for and remove blank columns
   For y = 1 To intCols
     If y > tbl.Columns.Count Then
        y = intCols
     Else
        intGotVal = 0
        For x = 1 To intRows
           If tbl.Cell(x, y).Range.Characters.Count > 1 Then
              intGotVal = intGotVal + 1
              x = intRows
           Else
```

21-14   Dreamboat On Word

```
            'Do Nothing
          End If
      Next x

      If intGotVal = 0 Then
         tbl.Columns(y).Delete
         y = y - 1
      Else
         'Do Nothing
      End If
    End If
  Next y

  'Reset column count and insert blank row
  'adding a column heading to each cell
  intCols = tbl.Columns.Count
  tbl.Rows(1).Select
  Selection.InsertRows 1
  For y = 1 To intCols
    tbl.Cell(1, y).Select
    Selection.Text = "Line" & y
  Next y

End Sub
```

Sample Macro 2: Fun Joke and an Old Macro Virus

This macro emulates an old macro virus that was around about five years ago.

Scenario

This doesn't serve any real purpose except to demonstrate how easy it is to create a macro "virus" and how to create a simple message box. The code does not otherwise affect the file; for instance, you'll still get the opportunity to save it. See Macro Security on page 21-1 for a further explanation of this code and Figure 21-1 to see the message box it creates.

Solution

Type all three pieces of the code below into the ThisDocument of your normal.dot file.

Macros and VBA

Code

```
Private Sub Document_Close()¶
¶
    MsgBox (Application.UserName &" is a big stupid jerk!")¶
End Sub¶
```

Sample Macro 3: Default Open View

Scenario

When you open Word documents, particularly from other people, they may open in Normal view or some other view that you don't prefer. This code opens ALL new and previously created files in Print Layout View (in '97, this is called Page Layout view).

Solution

Type all three pieces of the code below into the ThisDocument of your normal.dot file. If you have already created macros with these names, you simply take the "guts" of the code, that is—all but the first and last lines—and place them below any existing code, and BEFORE the End Sub.

> Note: *Document_Open in the normal.dot template is an event that occurs any time you open any document. Document_New in the normal.dot template is an event that occurs whenever you create a new document. Hence, this code does not open the Word application in the view that is coded, but will open documents and create new documents in the view that is coded.*

Code

```
Private Sub Document_New()¶
  Call SetView (wdPrintView¶)
End Sub¶
¶
Private Sub Document_Open()¶
  Call SetView (wdPrintView)¶
End Sub¶
¶
```

21-16 *Dreamboat On Word*

```
Private Sub SetView(ByVal iView As Integer)¶
  With ActiveDocument.ActiveWindow¶
    If .View.SplitSpecial = wdPaneNone Then¶
        .ActivePane.View.Type = iView¶
        .ActivePane.View.Zoom.PageFit = wdPageFitBestFit¶
    Else¶
        .View.Type = iView¶
        .View.Zoom.PageFit = wdPageFitBestFit¶
    End If¶
  End With¶
End Sub¶
```

Sample Macro 4: Clean All VBA Code From a Document

Scenario

You may have or receive files that contain code. You don't know what the code is for and you don't want the code in the document. Or you regularly record macros in documents and then later want to delete the code from the documents.

Solution

Rather than use the manual method of removing code, as described on page 21-5, you can use this code. The code must be placed in your normal.dot file so that it can be safely used on other files. You can use this code to clean code from any Word document except normal.dot. The document must be open when you run the macro. To run it, hit Tools→Macro→Macros and double-click the DeleteAllVBA macro.

Double-click Project (Normal) at the left and hit Insert→Module. In the code window for the new module, paste the following code:

Code
```
Public Sub DeleteAllVBA()¶
¶
Dim vbComp As Object¶
¶
```

Macros and VBA

```
For Each vbComp In
ActiveDocument.VBProject.VBComponents

  With vbComp
    If .Type = 100 Then
      .CodeModule.DeleteLines 1,
.CodeModule.CountOfLines
    Else
      ActiveDocument.VBProject.VBComponents.Remove
vbComp
    End If
  End With
Next vbComp

End Sub
```

22. Using Word with Other Applications

Most of these tricks are learned by trial and error. Does the fact that some of these tasks are difficult mean that they're bugs? No. But knowing how to search for the answers or workarounds can be tough. In this book I've provided every answer and/or workaround that I could.

Mail Merge Data Sources

Mail merges can be done with many file types other than Word documents. These are described in the chapter on Mail Merges, which begins on page 17-1.

Inserting Excel Objects

There are several methods of placing Excel files into documents:

1. Copy the cells in the Excel worksheet and paste them into the document.
   This method pastes the values only into Word in a Word table structure. No formulas are brought over, but you can now edit the data directly in Word.

2. Copy the cells in the Excel worksheet and paste them into the Word document using Edit→Paste Special→Paste Link. Using this method, you're actually connecting the Excel file to the Word document. Editing the contents of the cells through the Word document changes the contents in the Excel file and editing the contents of the Excel file changes the contents in the Word document. Formulas do work in this method.

Using Word with Other Applications

3. Copy the cells in the Excel worksheet and paste them into the Word document using Edit→Paste Special→As an Excel object.

   This method embeds the Excel object into the Word file, but no longer links it to the original Excel file. Changes must be made directly through the Word document, but formulas do work.

4. Choose Insert→Object then Select From File. This is the same as method 2.

Avoiding Problems

One of the most common problems that occur is that columns get cut off after pasting, and generally the columns are at the right of the pasted area.

Tip 54: Inserting Excel Objects Properly

There are some unwritten rules and common sense needed for inserting/pasting Excel objects without problems. They apply to inserting Excel objects into PowerPoint as well. They do not apply when using "paste" into Word, which pastes it as a Word table by default.

> What are the print settings in Excel? Don't expect an Excel file that is set to print to one page landscaped to fit into a portrait layout. Don't expect a worksheet that prints two pages wide to fit into one page width in Word. Don't expect to be able to copy three pages of Excel rows into one page in Word.

For best results, first remove all special print settings—like "center horizontally" and others—in Excel and save the file prior to copying the desired area.

➢ When choosing Insert→Object, be sure that the area that Excel sees as being used is reasonable. While you may only have 50 cells filled in the worksheet, Excel may see more cells being used.

In Excel, select cell A1 of the worksheet and hit Shift+Ctrl+End. If it selects empty rows and columns beyond your data area, you should first delete those rows and columns and save your file.

Converting Word Text to PowerPoint Presentations

Perhaps you create many PowerPoint presentations that are made primarily with text. A simple way to make a layout for your PowerPoint presentation using Word is to type slide titles and apply the Heading 1 style to them.

1. Type what will be your bulleted lists directly beneath the slide title text, and apply the Heading 2 style to them.

2. Then, hit File→Send to→ Microsoft PowerPoint. This automatically creates a presentation to which you can then apply any PowerPoint template and add your graphics.

Word as Your Outlook Email Editor

If you've never had any problems using this feature, please continue using it.

A word of caution to those who have not used Word as their email editor: You may find it is not worth the hassle. Some users have trouble from the outset; most have trouble because they believe that their recipients should see the format in which the email is sent.

Using Outlook Rich Text Format or Word as your email editor is a great idea if you only use inter-company email and everyone uses the same format. But the first time you email someone at a web-based email program like AOL, Yahoo or Hotmail, don't expect the recipient to see the email message in the same way that you sent it. Test out this feature before you get used to using it.

23. Important Word Files

There are several files that Word uses on your PC. As you use Word, these files become changed with settings that you have updated. If something happens to your hard drive, or if these files become corrupt, you may have to rebuild them. Learning their filenames, locations and what is stored in them helps you keep the your settings safe.

Files to Back Up

Some reasons you may want to back up important Word files:

> You are moving to a new PC at the same company or you are going to work for another employer.

> You want to share your settings with a coworker or with your own PC at home.

> Your hard drive crashes and becomes unrecoverable.

> Your IT department has informed you that they're going to update or reinstall your version of Word. Though many IT departments do take care of backing up these types of files, there are those who do not. Make it your responsibility, because you're the one that really loses if you don't.

If any of the above occurs, or rather, before any of the above occurs, you will want to make copies or backups of the following files, as well as all the regular documents you've created.

I've just read one of Microsoft's articles on this subject and they suggest you use a floppy disk. I don't condone the use of floppy disks for any reason.

Important Word Files

Here, I provide a description of what each file stores:

File Name	Description
Normal.dot	Each time you create a new document, a copy of normal.dot is provided for your use as the new document. Any settings you may have changed are stored in this file.
	Custom toolbar settings are stored in normal.dot as well. If you lose normal.dot, you'll have to set up all those toolbars/buttons again.
	Custom macros. If you've created custom macros that you use all the time, they'll be stored in normal.dot and you'll want to keep them safe.
	Normal.dot also stores your autotext entries. Some people would kill if they lost them.
Custom.dic	This is YOUR custom dictionary for Word. If you, from time to time, have added words to your dictionary during spell-check, then this is where those words are stored. This is particularly nice for Word users that work in medical offices or other jobs that require special terminology.
*.dot	Any other template files that you might have created. At work, many of us are provided a network share for our files. However, templates are by default stored on the hard drive. If for some reason you lose it, you won't have your custom templates anymore.
*.acl	Stores your Autocorrect entries, however, I strongly suggest you check the Microsoft Technet Knowledgebase for the complete story on backing up these files. There seem to be many anomalies.

Any of these files may become corrupt for no apparent reason. To protect yourself, back these files up to another location like a network drive or a coworker's PC or, at very least, another location on your own PC.

Suppose you work in a doctor's office and have added thousands of words to the dictionary. The Custom.dic file suddenly becomes corrupt. If you back this file up from time to time, you can likely delete the one that Word uses and replace it with the backup and recover some or most of the entries.

I mention backing up certain files several times throughout this book because I cannot stress enough how much efficiency you'll lose if you cannot remember every setting. Bottom line: If you've set Word up to your desired liking, keep a copy of these files somewhere safe.

Normal Dot Dot

Understanding normal.dot should help you to better understand Word. Normal.dot (endearingly referred to as Normal Dot Dot) is the default or global template that Word uses to create a blank document. Normal.dot is always in use when Word is open, even if you are using another template.

It is very common for normal.dot files to become what is referred to as corrupt. This doesn't necessarily mean that normal.dot has actually gone bad, but that it has inherited some behavior from the installation of another application, or contains information left over from someone trying to record a macro. They also store macros AND macro viruses.

When you launch Word, it looks for normal.dot and opens a copy of it. If your normal.dot is corrupt, it can cause Word to crash upon launching.

If Word cannot locate a normal.dot file, it creates a brand new one. When you first install Word, normal.dot is not installed with it. Uninstalling Word or Office does not delete normal.dot. These facts explain why reinstalling Office or Word often does not fix a problem with a corrupt or virus-infected normal.dot file. Your

Important Word Files

newly installed program finds normal.dot right where it was before and the problem you had still exists.

If you have never successfully run Word on your PC, then you may not have a normal.dot file and will have to look in some other direction for the cause of the problem.

Deleting or renaming normal.dot forces Word to create a new one.

The location of the normal.dot file that your version of Word uses can be found by opening Word and using the Tools→ Options, File locations tab. Double-click User templates. The path to normal.dot is in the lower area of the window under Folder name. If you're unable to see the whole path, hit your Home key on the keyboard.

Tip 55: Finding Normal.dot

To go to your normal.dot file, you can copy the path, hit Windows' Start→Run, paste the path into the box and hit Enter. This opens Windows Explorer to that folder.

Newer operating systems consider normal.dot to be a system file and therefore hide it. To search for it, you'll first have to tell Windows to show hidden files. Open Windows Explorer, hit Tools→Folder options. Choose the View tab and check the checkbox that says "Show hidden files and folders."

While you are there, you may want to uncheck "Hide file extensions for known file types." The text and checkbox selections vary slightly from one operating system to the next.

23-4   *Dreamboat On Word*

Normal.Dot Settings

You may have settings in your normal.dot that you would like to keep, such as customized toolbars and macros, while getting rid of normal.dot may be necessary due to corruption. So, instead of deleting normal.dot, it is recommended that you rename it to "abnormal.dot" or "normal1.dot." Then, you can use the Organizer to copy such things as macros and toolbars from the old template to the new one.

To learn how to use the Organizer, refer to page 4-2.

This page intentionally left blank.

24. Troubleshooting

People can be experts using Microsoft Word or any other application, but that does not mean that they know what to do when something goes wrong. Having this troubleshooting information is very useful, especially if Word were to suddenly start crashing on you in the middle of trying to meet a deadline.

Tip 56: A Caution About Troubleshooting

You may have an IT department or specialist where you work. Prior to performing any troubleshooting steps in any application or on your hard drive, you should get their permission! They may know of settings on the computers that could make the following instructions have catastrophic effects on the operation of your PC.

I cannot be held responsible for any negative ramifications due to following any of the troubleshooting steps that I provide here.

Cleaning Your Hard Drive

These instructions have been around for a long time. They've been updated from time to time to include new operating systems, but the basic instructions are the same. These instructions are followed by major software support firms that serve clients whose names you'll recognize no matter who you are. So, if they're good enough for the big guys, they'll work fine for you, too. I first made these instructions available through an auto-reply email and then finally posted them on the Internet.

Knowing how to clean your hard drive is probably the most important thing you can learn about your computer. Unfortunately, this information isn't provided with other basic information.

These steps are slightly more aggressive than the Disk Cleanup utilities provided by Windows.

Anyone is welcome to distribute this information freely and in any manner. Copy it, put your logo on it, pass it out to your friends, coworkers, etc. I think everyone should know how to maintain their PC without special software, which often causes more problems.

> Note: *In addition to the instructions below, it is imperative that you run virus-checking software and update the data files the moment new ones are available.*
>
> *Running spycheckers, such as Ad-Aware, is also a good move.*

Please read all of these steps carefully before implementing them. If you do not understand them, please do not continue to use them. We cannot be held responsible for any loss of data or equipment incurred as a result of performing these steps.

If the PC in question is your work PC, please check with members of your IT department, network desk, or help desk BEFORE performing these steps. Some companies have special setups and following these directions could cause problems.

1. Before you begin, shut down your PC and restart it. When it has completely restarted, close any programs that run automatically.

2. Hit Ctrl+Alt+Del and End Task on everything that appears in the list or Applications list EXCEPT Explorer and Systray.

3. Disable your screensaver if you use one.

Step 1: Delete trashy hard drive files.

These files are commonly referred to as "temp files".

1. Hit Start→Find→Files or Folders. (Use Start→ Search→Files or Folders on Windows ME, 2000 and 2002/XP.)

2. In the Named box, type:

   .tmp,~.*,*.chk

   > *Caution!* Be sure that you type the preceding exactly as it appears—double-check it to make sure it is exactly right. There are NO spaces between any of the characters.

3. The Look in box should have (C:) in it (or other hard drive[s]).

   > Note: *The Include Subfolders checkbox must be checked (not with Windows ME, 2000 or 2002/XP).*

4. Hit Find Now (or Search Now).

5. When the search is complete, hit Ctrl+A to select all of the files that appear and hit your delete key. Delete all files you possibly can, even if you get a warning. Some programs do not allow you to delete certain files. Do not be concerned if you can't delete files, just delete those that you can, even if you have to delete them one by one.

6. Send all the files to the recycle bin. Close the Find/Search window when you're all done.

Tip 57: Caution About File Extensions

There may be programs that actually use these file extensions, though I've never been told which ones they are. It's unlikely that you will have a problem, but this is why we advise NOT to empty your recycle bin for a few days.

Step 2: Delete Windows temp files.

1. Hit Start→Run and type `%temp%` and hit Enter. The contents of the Temp folder that your system uses by default should appear in the window.

2. Hit Ctrl+A on the keyboard to select everything in that folder and hit your delete key. Send the files to the recycle bin. Leave them there for at least a week to ensure that none of the files were needed. It's unlikely, however.

3. Close Windows Explorer.

Tip 58: Your Windows Temp Folder

The TEMP folder is a system folder. Do not use these folders to store your own files. Do not allow files to be stored here permanently.

Step 3: Delete temporary Internet files.

Step 3 is for Internet Explorer users only.

1. Open My Computer and note the Free space on your local drive by hitting View→Details. Now calculate a quantity of perhaps 10% of that amount. Close My Computer.

2. Open Internet Explorer and hit Tools→Internet Options. If you are having difficulty running Internet Explorer, right-click the shortcut and hit Properties to bring up the Internet Options dialog.

3. From the General tab, click on the Settings button. Set the amount of disk space for Internet Explorer to use to an amount that is equal to 10% of your hard drive space. This is just a rule of thumb and is not necessarily appropriate for everyone.

4. If you've got DSL or Cable, check the box "every visit to a page." If you've got phone-line Internet (DUN), check the box "every visit to a page" and groan while you do it. (There's no point in going to web sites and NOT viewing the most updated page. If you want to see the old page, then add it to your favorites and tell it you want it to be available offline.)

5. Hit Ok.

6. Click on the Delete files button. Do NOT click the checkbox for "delete all off-line content." Hit Ok. The history section has 20 days by default. Another rule of thumb—3 days ought to be enough.

7. Click on the Advanced tab. Scroll down to the Security area and check the box that says "empty temporary internet files when browser is closed." This keeps them from building up and taking all the space on your hard drive.

Troubleshooting

8. Hit Ok.

9. Close any and all open Windows.

Step 4: Cleanup by running Scandisk and Defrag.

Ideally, at this point, you'll empty your recycle bin. The first few times you perform these steps, however, you may not want to. Give it a week or so. When it's obvious that you did not delete anything important, empty your recycle bin.

1. Hit Start→Programs→Accessories→System tools→ Scandisk. Run it on the C: drive, choose Standard test, and choose to Automatically fix errors. Hit Start.

   > Note: *In Windows 2000 and 2002/XP, Scandisk is available by opening Windows Explorer, right-clicking the C:\ drive (or other hard drive) and choosing Properties. Then click the Tools tab and choose Error Checking.*

2. Hit Close. Hit Close again. Run a thorough scandisk once in a while if it makes you feel good or if you cannot complete a disk defragment (below).

Generally, Scandisk recommends that you run a thorough Scandisk when you need to. You can also run Scandisk by restarting the computer in MS-DOS mode (if this option is available with your version of Windows), typing "scandisk" at the DOS prompt, and then hitting Enter. This is particularly useful if you get the message "Scandisk has restarted 10 times."

> Note: *In newer versions of Windows, you may need to double-click My Computer, then right-click your hard drive. Hit Properties, and then the Tools tab. Choose Error-Checking, which has replaced Scandisk.*

> Note: *If you're using these steps to troubleshoot a specific problem, you can skip the next step, but you should definitely do it as soon as you can.*

1. Hit Start→ Programs→ Accessories→ System tools→ Disk Defragmenter. Run it on the C:\ drive or other hard drive. If you have never run Defrag before, or if you have not run it in a long time, this could take several hours! You may need to hit the details button to watch your hard drive get defragged.

2. When it's done, hit the Yes button to exit the disk defragmenter and restart your PC.

> Note: *In newer versions of Windows, you may need to double-click My Computer,* **then** *right-click your hard drive. Hit Properties, and then the Tools tab. Choose Disk Defragmenter from there.*

Physical Cleanup

Every so often someone is looking to clean his or her external PC components.

I've been successful using the following methods for years. Of course, I can't be responsible for any damages you might incur by using these methods.

Instructions

> *Caution!* Always turn your PC and components off completely before cleaning.

1. I use liquid bleach cleaner. Just dampen a paper towel with the cleaner and wipe. When it is clean, wipe down thoroughly with a water-dampened paper towel. Never put the cleaner or water right on your PC; always apply it with a paper towel that is not dripping wet!!

> *Caution!* If the cleaner or water drips or runs while you're wiping, you're using too much and could ruin your PC.

2. Turn your keyboard upside down (take it outside like you would a dirty rug). Then, use canned, pressurized air to blow out the dust from underneath the keys.

3. Turn your mouse upside down and unscrew the plate. Take the ball out, remove any dust or buildup from the little black "rolling pins," gently blow the open area out or again use pressurized air; put the pieces back together.

Troubleshooting Word

Many people, when having a problem running Word, immediately reinstall Office. For many problems, reinstalling Office does not help. Here are the steps you should take, in order. They apply to all versions of Microsoft Word on Windows 95 and new versions of Windows.

Tip 59: Recovering Lost Toolbars & Menus

> If you have lost your toolbars in Word, take only Step 3. If that does not work, then take Step 5, which always works for lost toolbars.

Step 1. Ensure that Word, and not the document, is the problem.

If you experience the behavior in any file, and particularly in a new file, then you know that the problem lies with Word. If you cannot duplicate the behavior in another file, it is likely a corrupt document.

Troubleshooting

The steps to troubleshoot corrupt documents can be found in Word Document Troubleshooting on page 24-14.

Step 2. Clean up your hard drive.

Keeping your hard drive clean is of the utmost importance, particularly when attempting to troubleshoot other problems. Complete instructions are provided on page 24-1.

Step 3. Rename normal.dot.

This is one of the most common fixes for Microsoft Word application problems.

1. With Word closed, find and rename the normal.dot file on your system. If there is more than one, rename them all.

2. If you cannot find normal.dot or if you are on a network, you can find where your normal.dot is stored by checking under User Templates on the Tools→Options, File Locations tab.

3. If you do not have "permission" to rename normal.dot, check with your network administrator or internal helpdesk (should apply only on some PCs at work, not home users).

4. After you have renamed normal.dot, launch Word. If the problem is not resolved, move to step 4.

See page 23-3 for more information on finding and working with the normal.dot file.

Step 4. Check the Startup folder.

1. With Word closed, use Windows Explorer to find the Word Startup folder, usually:

    C:\Program Files\Microsoft\Office\Word\Startup

Dreamboat On Word

Troubleshooting

2. Be sure that there are no files in this folder that you did not intentionally put in there yourself.

Word has the STARTUP folder and Excel has the XLSTART folder. Files in either of these folders are automatically opened when you launch the respective program.

Tip 60: Programs That Interfere With Word

Some programs can interfere with the smooth and error-free operation of Word.

Newer versions of Norton Antivirus have a setting that can cause Word to slow down significantly upon opening of a file. This is because you have a setting in Norton to scan all Office files for viruses upon opening them.

If Norton is doing its job, files that contain viruses should have been caught on your PC long before you had the opportunity to open it. However, you should always download files from the web before opening them on your PC so that your virus checker software has an opportunity to scan it BEFORE you open the file.

Adobe Acrobat, PDF Writer and Visio are programs that can interfere with Word. While some people use these options all the time, others do not and may not understand certain error messages.

If Word is not working properly for you, you will often find the exact error message in the Microsoft Technet Knowledgebase at http://support.microsoft.com.

Step 5. "Dump" the registry key.

Ensure that Word is closed.

You'll be opening the Windows Registry Editor. You may have read that this is dangerous and that can be true. Normally, we would backup your registry to be safe, but we're going to rename only your Word key.

In the unlikely event that your Word application becomes totally disabled, you can simply delete the new Word key that gets created in the registry and rename the old one back to its original name. If you follow the instructions exactly, you will not have a problem.

1. Start→Run and type: regedit

2. Hit your Enter key. As you might browse folders in Windows Explorer, browse to the appropriate path:

   For Word 97:
   hkey_current_user\software\microsoft\office\8.0\word

   For Word 2000:
   hkey_current_user\software\microsoft\office\9.0\word

   For Word 2002/XP:
   hkey_current_user\software\microsoft\office\10.0\word

   > *Caution!* If you are unable to find this folder, or do not understand how to find it, then you should stop here and get support over the phone or in person.

3. Once you have found the path, right-click the Word folder, hit Rename and rename it to OldWord.

4. Hit Enter and then exit the Registry Editor; relaunch Word. If this still has not resolved the problem, move on to Step 6.

Step 6. Uninstall, Erase and Reinstall Office.

Uninstall using Add/Remove programs in the Control Panel.

1. Start→Settings→Control panel. Select Office and then choose Remove.

2. Run Eraser 97 or 2000, as appropriate. Instructions and downloads can be found at:

    Office 97:
    http://support.microsoft.com/support/kb/articles/Q176/8/23.ASP

    Office 2000:
    http://support.microsoft.com/support/kb/articles/Q219/4/23.ASP

    Office 2002/XP:
    There is no Eraser program available, nor is it necessary, for Office 2002/XP.

    Note: Prior to installing or reinstalling any significant program, be sure that there are no programs running in the background that could interfere with the installation.

3. Hit Ctrl+Alt+Del to bring up your task list. One by one, end task for all items EXCEPT Explorer and Systray.

4. Reinstall Office using the installation disks.

Troubleshooting Files

Because Word files fall under these General File Troubleshooting rules, I include the rules as they apply to any kind of file and not just to Word files.

General File Troubleshooting

One trick that might work with any of the files is to hold down the left shift key while you double-click to open the file. Why? This keeps automatic Visual Basic code from running and certain other auto-commands, which may be causing the error.

Similarly, this sometimes works if you're getting an error starting a program—hold the shift key down while you launch the program.

Another trick that works is to open a file from a higher version of a SIMILAR program. You might not always get the results you want, but you'll be able to edit it and save it back. Sometimes, a different program doesn't "interpret the corruption" of the document. For instance, try opening a Word 97 file with Wordperfect 8; try opening an Excel 97 file with Lotus 1-2-3 Millenium.

If you're at work and store your files on a network drive, you can always retrieve a copy of your file from the previous network backup. Depending on the size of your company and the response time of your helpdesk, this can take anywhere from one to twenty-four hours or even longer.

If your file resides on a floppy, always try the following, no matter how ridiculous they sound:

> Take the floppy out and blow on the areas (I hear you laughing, but it's true!) around the openings.

> Try copying the file from the floppy to a location on the hard drive.

> Try running scandisk and defrag on the floppy drive.

> Lastly, take it to another PC and attempt to open it. If the latter works, you might want to have your floppy drive checked out.

If none of the other troubleshooting helps, look for temporary files on your hard drive as discussed in Step 2 on page 24-4. See if any of these files are of significant size, even similar in size to your original file.

If you crashed your PC and lost your file/changes, check these temporary files for a date and time near to the time of your crash. If you find a likely candidate file, you can rename it to the appropriate file extension, i.e., DOC for a Word document, and attempt to open it. I have seen a lot of work recovered using this method.

Word Document Troubleshooting

If you open a file and, while scrolling or printing, Word locks up or gives a protection fault:

1. Open the file and hit the Show/Hide button on your standard toolbar.

2. With your cursor at the beginning of your document, hit Ctrl+End.

3. Hold down the left shift key and use the right arrow key to deselect any extra paragraph markers at the bottom of your document. If there is only one, you may want to go ahead and deselect the last sentence of your document—you can always retype it.

4. Hit the copy button or Ctrl+C to copy the document. Paste it into a new, blank document and save it.

Generally, if the file size has reduced considerably, you've probably gotten rid of the corruption. You may need to reset certain formatting, such as landscaped pages. Hit File→Properties and then the General tab to view the file size in the original document, and then in the new document; or just go to Windows Explorer to compare sizes.

If your document still throws errors, most likely there is a graphic or other object in the document that is corrupt. You can copy and paste pieces of your document to a new document, saving the new document each time, until you get the error. Then you can copy the rest of the document—all but that portion—into the new document.

Another trick is to open a blank document, hit enter at least once, then hit Insert→File and insert your "bad" file into the new file. This method also removes protection from a document that has been protected using Tools→Protect Document, even if it's got a password. It does not work to open a password-protected file.

If all else fails, you can always try using "Recover text from any file" option under the file types. This generally recovers only the text of your document, as well as some metadata.

Other Common Issues

While Word has its issues, so do the people who use it. People love to blame the software for problems that turn out to originate

Troubleshooting

somewhere between the chair and the keyboard. Now that chair and keyboard might not have been yours, but the issue may have landed in your lap.

Here are just a few of them.

Cannot Spell Check

There are known issues as to why spell checking won't work. However, probably more than fifty percent of the time, it's because of something a user did. The best thing you can do is hit Select All (Ctrl+A) in your document, then go to Tools→ Language→Set Language. Be sure the Do not check spelling or grammar check box is NOT checked.

After you have done that, you must then go to Tools→Options, Spelling and Grammar tab, and hit the Recheck Document button. This makes Word behave as if the document had never been checked.

Cannot Change Text

The document may be protected and you're not supposed to change the text. If you receive a document from someone and you can only enter text in certain areas, please don't attempt to change the rest of the text in the document. People painstakingly create forms for your use. If you unprotect the document, you may make your completed form useless to the person who sent it to you.

Appendix A

Windows Keyboard Shortcuts

Ctrl+	Performs this action in Word
A	Selects the entire document, the contents of a textbox or the entire header or footer; depending on where the cursor resides when Ctrl+A is selected. Equivalent to Edit→Select All.
B	Bolds selected text or turns bold on for text that is not yet typed at the insertion point.
C	Copies selected text or object to the Office Clipboard.
D	Brings up the Font formatting dialog box. Equivalent to Format→Font.
E	Centers the paragraph of text at the insertion point.
F	Brings up the Find tab of the Find and Replace dialog box. Equivalent to Edit→Find.
G	Brings up the Go to tab of the Find and Replace dialog box. Equivalent to Edit→Go To.
H	Brings up the Replace tab of the Find and Replace dialog box. Equivalent to Edit→Replace.
I	Italicizes selected text or turns italics on for text that is not yet typed at the insertion point.
J	Fully justifies the selected paragraph(s) or turns that setting on at the insertion point.
K	Brings up the Insert→Hyperlink dialog box.
L	Left-aligns the selected paragraph(s) or turns that setting on at the insertion point.
M	Increases paragraph indentation to the next tab setting.
N	Brings up a new document.
O	Brings up the File→Open dialog box.

Appendix A

Ctrl+	Performs this action in Word
P	Prints the active document to the printer without the Print dialog box.
Q	Returns the paragraph spacing of selected text to zero points before and after, and to single spaced paragraphs.
R	Right-aligns the selected paragraph(s) or turns that setting on at the insertion point.
S	Saves the active document to its current file name or, if not previously saved, brings up the Save As dialog box. Equivalent to File→Save.
T	Creates a hanging indent format and takes the insertion point to the next tab setting.
U	Underlines selected text or turns underlining on for text that is not yet typed at the insertion point.
V	Pastes an item from the clipboard to the insertion point. Equivalent to Edit→Paste
W	Closes the active document. Equivalent to File→Close.
X	Cuts the selected text or object and stores it on the clipboard. Equivalent to Edit→Cut.
Y	Redo. Repeats the last command.
Z	Undo. Undoes the last command.

Recommended Settings in Word

Here I make recommendations on Word's settings. If I do not list a specific setting, it means that I believe you should make your own choice or leave it set to the default setting. In no way does the omission of the setting mean that the setting itself is not important.

Tab	Option	Setting	Comments
View	Highlight	Checked	Shows text that has been marked with the Highlight feature.
View	Bookmarks	Unchecked	Check this option if you develop templates and other documents.
View	Status Bar	Checked	There are often important messages in the status bar that you shouldn't miss.
View	Field codes	Unchecked	Turn this on when you're trying to see what's behind your field codes. Alt+F9 toggles this off and on for you.
View	Field shading	Always	We prefer to have this set to Always. When working in forms using the Forms toolbar, this makes it much easier to follow what you're doing.

Appendix A

Tab	Option	Setting	Comments
View	Formatting Marks	All	When you have the Show/Hide button turned on, it shows the non-printing characters that are checkmarked. Because we always suggest having the Show/Hide button on, All should be selected.
General	Background Pagination	Checked	Because we recommend using Page Layout or Print Layout as your view, this must be turned on.
General	Confirm Conversion at Open	Checked	If you never work with other document types except Word, there is no need to turn this on.
General	Auto-create drawing canvas	Unchecked	I don't see the point.
Edit	[all]	Default	Use the default settings or set as desired. I'm not crazy about smart tags and tracking formatting.
Print	Background Printing	Unchecked	In some versions, this is the reason that the Page X of Y feature doesn't provide proper sequential numbering.

A-4   Dreamboat On Word

Tab	Option	Setting	Comments
Save	Allow Fast Saves	Unchecked	This actually saves your file in small pieces that you've edited, as opposed to saving your entire document. It's also the reason you may see many temporary files while you work in a single document.
Save	Prompt to Save Normal template	As desired	Word macro viruses may attach themselves to your normal.dot template. Checking this setting may alert you to the fact that you have a macro virus. However, this method generally is unreliable because you'll get the prompt for many, many other reasons. Always use an updated Antivirus program so you don't need to count on settings like this.
User Info	[All]	Complete these fields	Among other things, when you request a return address on an envelope, it uses this data.
Compatibility Options	[All]	[All]	You should review these so that you can become aware of the many settings available. Generally, the default settings are fine, but some desktop publishers will appreciate the ability to choose some of the settings.

Appendix A

Tab	Option	Setting	Comments
File Locations	[All]	[All]	Again, change as desired, but you should be aware of these settings.
Security	[All]	[All]	This tab is new in XP/2002, and contains options that we could not previously set. You should become familiar with them.
Spelling & Grammar	[All]	[All]	As desired.
Tracked Changes	[All]	[All]	As desired.

Glossary

Term	Definition
Code	Visual Basic for Applications code. See VBA and Macro.
Document	Document often refers not only to Word documents, but other types of documents as well, such as spreadsheets or presentations.
Embedded	An object that resides within a Word document, instead of as a separately linked file, is "embedded". The alternative is to link the object or file.
Field	Regarding Word, fields are areas in the document that do not necessarily contain text, but require actions to create them. Fields are generally updateable. Some fields are form fields, mail merge fields, cross-references, bookmarks and calculations.
Forms	Documents that you can fill out, electronically or by hand. When we refer to forms in Word, we are generally referring to the creation of documents that can be filled out electronically.
Graphic	Any kind of file that is a picture, whether embedded in the document or contained in its own separate file. Other words that can mean the same thing: picture, image.
Insertion point	The location where text appears when you begin typing. You can move the insertion point with directional arrow keys on the keyboard or left-click your mouse at the desired location.
Macro	Macros are used to create a set of commands or tasks to be performed automatically. Macros are created using VBA code. See VBA.
Office clipboard	Prior to Office 2000, the Office programs used the Windows clipboard. Both clipboards temporarily store items that are copied. With Office 2000, Office brought in their own clipboard that is specific to only the Office applications, including Outlook. Many people don't like the intrusive behavior of the new Office clipboard.

Appendix A

Term	Definition
Screen shot/ Screen capture	An image of what you see on your screen. To get one, hit the Print Screen button on your keyboard. This copies an image of your monitor screen to the Windows clipboard. Simply go to a Word document or other application file and hit Paste. To capture only the "active window," such as an application window, press and hold the Alt key while you hit the Print Screen button. I personally prefer to use a program called SnagIt from www.TechSmith.com for this purpose because it creates a cleaner image than Windows does.
TOC	Table of contents
Toggle	Like a light switch, some toolbar buttons and other Word settings are "toggled" on and off. This means you use the same toolbar button or keyboard shortcut to turn the option on as you do to turn it off. To start typing bolded text, hit Ctrl+B. Type your text. When you're done, hit Ctrl+B again to "toggle" it off.
Trouble-shoot	I believe this term is commonly misunderstood. Troubleshooting is not generally a one-step process, but may have many steps. If you solicit someone's help in fixing your Word application, for example, don't expect a one-line response. Troubleshoot could easily be replaced with "Try this and if it doesn't work, try that..." and so forth. Generally, the easiest task with the least ramifications is performed first.
VBA	Visual Basic for Applications. This is a mini-version of Visual Basic (VB). While VB is used to create programs "from scratch," Microsoft has included VBA with certain applications. In my book, I use the terms "VBA," "macro," and "code" almost interchangeably.
VBE	Visual Basic Editor. This is the application window for VBA. See VBA.

Index

AutoCorrect	3-17
AutoFormat	5-6
AutoText	
Creating	4-4
Naming	4-5
Sharing	4-5
Backing Up Files	23-1
Bookmarks	
Automatic	16-4
Borders	11-1
Headers/Footers	11-5
Page Borders	11-2
Table	11-3
Text	11-3
Breaks	
Column	13-3
Continuous Section	13-3
Even-Page Section	13-4
Next-Page Section	13-3
Odd-Page Section	13-4
Page	13-1
Text Wrapping	13-3
Bullets and Numbering	10-2
Fixing	10-3
Lists	10-2
Outlines	10-4
Reset	10-1
Business Card	15-9
Calculations	4-10
Columns	
Tables	12-10
Cross-References	5-7, 16-5
Document Map	4-1
Drawing Canvas	19-1
Endnotes	See Footnotes

Index

Envelopes **5-8**
Equation Editor **4-9**
Excel, Inserting Objects **22-1, 22-2**
File Size, Keeping Down **19-3, 19-4**
Find and Replace **4-6**
Fonts **6-1**
   Default, set 6-3
   Formatting 6-3
   Hidden Text 6-4
   Symbols 6-5
   Web Fonts 6-2
   WordPerfect 6-5

Footnotes
   Format 16-3

Format Painter **4-11**
   Bullets and Numbering, fixing 10-3

Forms
   Click and Type Fields 18-3
   Field Shading 18-1
   Fields 18-4
   Fill-In 18-4
   Hyperlinks 18-12
   Macro Button Fields 18-1
   Protecting 18-10
   Spell checking 18-11
   Tables, using with 12-9
   User Forms 18-12

Graphics
   Behind Text 19-7
   Drawing Canvas 19-1
   Drawing Tips 19-3
   In Front of Text 19-7
   In Line With Text 19-6
   Square 19-7
   Styles 9-17
   Tables, using with 12-9
   Tight 19-7
   WordArt 19-2

Hard Drive, Cleaning **24-1, 24-7**
Headers/Footers

Index

Borders 11-5
Hyperlinks **16-5**
   Forms 18-12
   Other Document Types, link to 16-7

Indexing **5-6**
Keyboard Settings **3-1**
Labels **5-9**
   Table to Text 12-12

Layouts
   Booklets 15-4
   Newsletter 15-4
   Two-Sided 15-5

Leaders **8-11**
Letterhead **15-8**

Links
   Documents Sharing Sections 15-7

Macros
   Defined 21-1
   Record 21-8
   Security 21-3

Macros, Samples
   Default Open View 21-16
   Labels to Data 21-12
   Message Box 21-15

Mail Merge
   Conditional Merges 17-5
   Data Sources 17-2
   Main Documents 17-1
   Printing 17-8
   Queries 17-3

Master/Subdocuments **5-1**
   Styles 9-11
   Troubleshooting 5-4, 5-5

Menus **3-1**
   Customizing 3-7
   Default 3-1
   Reset 3-10

Normal.dot **23-3**
   Finding 23-4

Index

Numbering Lists .... *See* Bullets and Numbering
Option Settings **3-16**
Organizer **4-2**
   Styles 9-9
Outlines **10-4**
   Formatting 10-4
Outlook, Word as Email Editor **22-4**
Page Borders **11-2**
Page Numbers
   Custom 14-3
   Formatting, placement 14-2
   Inserting 14-1
Paragraph **7-1**
   Indents 7-2, 7-5
   Spacing Between 7-2, 7-6
PowerPoint, Converting Word to use in **22-3**
Printing
   Blank Pages 20-3
   Print Codes 20-3
   Printing Selected Ranges 20-1
   Troubleshooting 20-3
Protection
   Forms 18-10
Shading **11-1**
Shortcut Keys **3-11**
   Windows 3-11
   Word 3-12
Shortcuts
   Styles 9-16
Signature Lines **12-9**
Sorting
   Without a Table 12-3
Spell Checker
   Troubleshooting 9-15
Spell Checking
   Forms 18-11

Index

Stationary	**15-8**
Styles	**9-1**
Custom, create	9-7
Editing	9-7
Format Painter	4-11
Graphics	9-17
Organizing	9-9
Shortcuts	9-16
Troubleshooting	9-11
Symbols	**6-5**
Table of Contents	
Creating from Styles	9-8
Tables	
Borders	11-3
Calculations	4-10
Converting to/from Text	12-11
Creating	12-1
Facts and Uses	12-5, 12-7, 12-9, 12-10
Forms, using with	18-8, 18-9
Merged Cells	12-10
Tabs	**8-1**
Bar Tab	8-9
Center-Aligned	8-6
Data File, turning into a	8-4
Decimal-Aligned	8-8
Default Settings	8-2
Leaders	8-11
Left-Aligned	8-6
Right-Aligned	8-7
Setting	8-10
Taskbar	**3-11**
Templates	
Business Cards	15-9
Convert to Document	15-2
Layouts	15-4, 15-5
Letterhead	15-8
Outlines	10-5
Shortcuts	15-2
Styles, creating new	9-1
Styles, troubleshooting	9-12
Workgroups, working with	15-3
Toolbars	**3-1, 18-4, 19-3**

Dreamboat On Word I-5

Index

Customizing...3-7
Default...3-1
Reset..3-10

Troubleshooting
Any File..24-13
Bullets and Numbering...10-3
Documents...24-14
Master/Subdocument..9-12
Normal.dot..23-3
Printing..20-3
Spell Checker..9-15
Spell checking...24-16
Styles...9-11
Tables..12-5, 12-10
Tables, Text...7-4
Text, Unable to Change..24-16
Word...24-8

Views
Default..5-7
Outline View..4-12

Viruses..**21-3**
Avoiding...21-2
Cleaning Document...21-5

I-6   *Dreamboat On Word*

also from
Holy Macro! Books...

Bill Jelen and Joseph Rubin

MR EXCEL
ON EXCEL

EXCEL 97   EXCEL 2000   EXCEL 2002

"The real Excel bible! The best practical book on Excel with absolutely no useless filler."

Microsoft Excel is an incredibly feature-rich product. Far too many people are introduced to Excel through a trial-by-fire basis when they discover they need it for their job. They learn the basics, but continue doing things the hard way. This book gives them tips that can cut **hours and hours** from their routine tasks.

ISBN 0-9724258-3-7 $35.95 480 Pages

Coming March 2004 from Holy Macro! Books...

Kathy Jacobs ON POWERPOINT

"If you do PowerPoint, do this book. Go from blocked to brilliant in minutes!"

ISBN 0-9724258-6-1
380 Pages
Available March 2004

ALSO FROM HOLY MACRO! BOOKS

Shop for these titles at your local bookstore or order direct.
E-Mail: store@MrExcel.com   **Mail:** 13386 Judy, Uniontown OH 44685
Online: http://www.MrExcel.com   **Fax:** (707) 220-4510

Qty	Title	Price	Total
	Dreamboat ON WORD By Anne Troy The real word on Word. It is so much easier when you know all the secrets and avoid the pitfalls! An honest, must-have resource. ISBN 0-9724258-4-5 (256 pages – 2003)	$19.95	
	Mr Excel ON EXCEL By Bill Jelen and Joseph Rubin, CPA Designed for the person who can perform the basics with their eyes closed all day but has been too busy to learn all the techniques to make the use of Excel far more efficient. ISBN 0-9724258-3-7 (480 pages – 2003)	$35.95	
	Holy Macro! It's 1,600 Excel VBA Examples (CD) By Hans Herber and Bill Jelen This is an amazing resource for anyone who has to write VBA programs for Excel. Contains every snippet of Excel VBA code you should ever need. ISBN 0-9724258-1-0 (1600 pages – 2002)	$89.00	
	Excel Knowledge Base (CD) By the Readers of MrExcel.com From 1999 – 2002, the original message board at MrExcel.com provided over 12,000 answers to questions posed by MrExcel.com readers. We've taken the original message threads, categorized them, and compiled them into a completely searchable CD-ROM. ISBN 0-9724258-2-9 (12,700 pages – 2002)	$49.00	
	Guerilla Data Analysis Using Microsoft Excel De-mystifies the arduous task of dealing with downloaded data. Allows you to unleash the power of Excel and get the world's most popular analytical tools to work for you – instead of the other way around. ISBN 0-9724258-0-2 (108 pages – 2002)	$19.95	

Check for new titles at www.HolyMacroBooks.com

Sales Tax: Ohio residents add 6.25% sales tax
Shipping: U.S. Shipping included. International, add $5 per order.
Payment: Check to "MrExcel" or VISA/MC/American Express
Bulk Orders: Save 40% when you order 6 or more of any one title.

Name: _____
Address: _____
City, State, Zip _____
Email: _____
Card # _____ Exp: _____